MW01520104

God, Pandas, and a Stethoscope

PAUL SCHUSTER

Published by PAUL SCHUSTER, 2023.

Table of Contents

To Michelle, my love, my wife, my best friend,

and fellow pilgrim in the delightful adventure of life.

Introduction

My darling wife, Michelle, and I, along with our four little ones, landed in China on a sweltering August evening. I had procured a job as a staff veterinarian at the Chengdu Zoo in Sichuan province several months earlier, and we had arrived to start our big adventure together.

The first few weeks were a hailstorm of new impressions and experiences, but I carved out the time to write them down, knowing that in a few months, the strange and exotic would become trite and ordinary.

This journaling continued at the zoo, where the bizarre was so common that it seemed a shame not to keep track of it.

This book also includes reflections. One of the great joys of my life is to marvel at the ingenious hand of God in the creatures he has made. The diversity of animals at a zoo seemed to highlight his inexhaustible inventiveness. Having studied comparative anatomy in some depth, I had become convinced that the marvelous creatures I was working on did not come to exist as the result of some random cosmic sneeze, but through the skilled hand of a brilliant Creator.

During my studies at university, though I was raised as a Christian, I determined to open my mind to every logical worldview, including the nonexistence of God. Several of my professors were ardent atheists with a great dislike for all things religious and a special vehemence for the God of the Christians. They determined to convince any who entered their halls of learning that God was a fantasy and that evolution, guided by statistical probability, caused our existence.

However, as I studied embryology, pathology, and the many subjects I delved into during my six-year sojourn in vet school, I became more and more convinced that such complexity, beauty, and infinite detail as we see in the animal world could not have come about by chance. It was deliberately designed and created. But that does not mean I gave up on science. Rather, science allowed me to see the staggering beauty and intricacy of the creatures I studied with renewed fascination.

In the book of Proverbs, Solomon, the famously wise king said, "It is the glory of God to conceal a thing: but the honour of kings is to search out a matter" (Proverbs 25:2). God has concealed many of his miracles deep in the bodies, functions, and behaviours of the animals he made. I have searched out some of these matters, and though I am not a king (or even remotely royal) it has truly been an honour to do so. Understanding how the various animals functioned gave me glimpses into the creative mind of God, and as I learned, I marveled. David said it well in Psalm 110: "Praise the LORD. I will extol the LORD with all my heart in the council of the upright and in the assembly. Great are the works of the LORD; they are pondered by all who delight in them. Glorious and majestic are his deeds, and his righteousness endures forever. He has caused his wonders to be remembered; the LORD is gracious and compassionate."

It is by his grace that we may "remember his wonders," and experience his glory. As David said, "When I consider your heavens, the work of your fingers, the moon and the stars, which you have set in place, what is man that you are mindful of him, the son of man that you care for him?" (Psalm 8:3-6).

Though we are infinitely small in the economy of God, his love is so vast that he has called us to see him in what he created. Romans 1:20 says, "For since the creation of the world, God's invisible qualities—his eternal power and divine nature—have been clearly seen, being understood from what has been made, so that men are without excuse." Being without excuse, we come to God as his creation, seeking a relationship with the one who made us. But God needed to take the first step. He sent his Son to bear the consequence of our sin, in order to bridge the gulf that separates us from our Creator. Jesus willingly died so that we might delight in the glory of God forever. God stands before us, opening his arms to us, welcoming us to know him in all his majesty. At the zoo, I have had the incredible privilege of climbing onto the lap of the great Creator, and being allowed a small peek into his sketchbook.

Monkey Trouble

Sweat pasted the shirt to my back as I hurried through the steamy heat. Ornately carved wooden doors and tiled temple roofs slipped by unnoticed as my companion and I ran along the winding paths of the Buddhist temple, a life slipping away in our arms. We ran like soldiers in a frantic parade—shoulder to shoulder, our upper bodies composed and proper, carrying our load in stiff outstretched arms, our legs pumping us along. Small groups of wide-eyed worshippers stared as we hurried by. "You will never guess what I saw when I burned incense today," they would say when they got home.

It started just after lunch, during that sleepy stretch of the day, when my colleagues in the vet department were draped over their desks in snoring heaps. My stomach had finished its argument with the spicy canteen lunch, and I was engrossed in an internet article on elephant hormones when my new friend, Dr. Lin, broke the calm and scurried past the open door of my office. Intrigued, I pushed back my chair and peered down the concrete hall to see him duck into the drug room.

He emerged holding the fancy imported dart gun and hurried to meet the others, who were stumbling sleepily from their offices, in the small conference room. I had only been working at the zoo a few months, so there was much that was unfamiliar, but scurrying about during afternoon naptime was highly unusual and needed to be investigated.

I joined my colleagues in the meeting room, walking slowly to hide my excitement. Director Li, elegant as always in her high-heeled shoes and summer dress, stood in the centre of the group. She seemed more appropriately attired for an evening soiree than the muck of elephant cages and deer yards, but she was very much a professional and held a firm, but kind, grip on the department. She explained the situation.

Some of the younger staff were leaning in to listen while the more senior members rested against a wall, hoping for a little more shut-eye. I joined the younger crowd and leaned in. Straining to catch more of the local dialect, I understood just enough to learn that a monkey had escaped. Apparently, during the keepers' afternoon nap, a large male Tibetan Macaque had taken advantage of a rusty cage latch and had gone sightseeing. Our park-like zoo was wrapped around a sprawling Buddhist temple complex, and, seeing as his cage was conveniently placed next to the temple wall, he made that his first stop.

"Escapes like this happen sometimes," the junior assistant beside me whispered, noticing my raised eyebrows. "But they rarely get beyond the wall."

Dr. Lin and I, as the youngest and most spry members of the veterinary team, were chosen to recapture the runaway, along with the macaque keeper who was shifting nervously beside me chewing his lower lip. He was distressed. I was giddy.

As the three of us made our way down the hall of the vet department, Dr Lin turned to me.

"Here, you use this," he said as he handed me the imported dart gun.

This gun, with its shiny metal barrel and finely crafted hand grip, was kept in a locked cupboard and had been given as a special gift from the National Zoo in Washington, DC. It was a weapon in the truest sense of the word, could shoot accurately over a great distance, and came complete with expertly crafted darts, which could be loaded with potent drugs. It was powered by a high-pressure CO_2 cartridge.

"I'll use this," Dr. Lin said, holding up a white plastic tube. It cost twenty-five cents at the local hardware store, used darts that we crafted ourselves by melting together cheap syringes, and was powered by his lungs.

Embarrassingly, the previous few months had taught me he was more accurate with his plastic tube than I was with the fancy gun, so offering me the better weapon was a generous, face-saving gesture, and put us on more equal footing. If he had handed me the blow tube and kept the gun for himself, I might as well have stayed behind. Dr. Lin was becoming a genuine friend.

We stuffed our shirt pockets with anaesthetic darts and jogged the considerable distance to the temple gate, nodding to the agent at the ticket counter as we hurried past.

The ancient temple grounds were too vast to cover at a run, so we slowed our pace and made our way along the wide gravel paths, mercifully shaded by towering gingko trees. We peered down dark alleys between ornate buildings and up into the lofty branches. Cicadas screeched in the treetops, and the pungent scent of burning sandalwood wafted by as we passed the huge brass urns that held the incense sticks. Groups of monks floated about in saffron sarongs, and little clusters of shuffling local tourists milled about in the shade of the trees. But nowhere was there a crowd worthy of a renegade monkey.

Deep in the temple complex, near the vegan cafeteria, and just behind a huge brass incense burner, a delighted gathering of screaming children pointed to a rooftop. We were close. Beady black eyes peered cautiously over the roof tiles at the peak of a building and then disappeared. I joined the mob of screaming children as we ran around only to watch a stubby tail slip over the crest of the next building. This would not be easy. Macaques are fast—and scared ones even more so.

"Let's split up so we can cover more ground," Dr. Lin said, and then, with an impish grin he added, "but if you see him first, you'd better not miss!"

We parted ways, and I began to sneak around on my own, urged on by the thrill of the hunt and the pressure of competition. I was determined not to come up empty-handed.

Creeping around a flaky red wall, I was confronted by an excited young monk in yellow robes who interrupted my covert operation, bouncing and gesticulating wildly.

"I saw him, I saw him!" he screamed before disappearing down a winding path.

I raced to catch up to the flying sandals and billowing robes. The monkey made its way along the base of a wall and then, just as we got close, slipped under it through a concrete drain.

"We can get in there," the novice monk yelled, pointing excitedly to a nearby door. "We just need to go through the teachers' quarters."

Clearly, this monkey hunt was a highlight in his serene existence, and he was having a hard time controlling his excitement. However, as a monk in training, he took a deep breath and slowed his pace to assume the serene composure he would need if he was going to disturb a senior Buddhist teacher. Calmly and respectfully, we approached a simple wooden door. The novice knocked gently and waited... Nothing. Not a sound. Zen-like silence.

"Teacher?" the novice ventured gently, realizing that he might be interrupting his mentor during meditation.

No answer.

"Teacher?" he tried again, a little louder.

We waited. I pictured our monkey grinning gleefully as he raced on, thrilled that his plot to stall us with dawdling Buddhist monks was working so well. It was hard to resist banging frantically on the door.

Finally, after an agonizing wait, we heard the slow shuffle of sandaled feet. The door creaked open and a short, balding, sleepy-eyed monk squinted in the daylight. Getting up at five a.m. for chanting must have been wearing on him, so he had been enjoying a little afternoon nap. After our profuse apology for disturbing him, he ushered us sleepily through the plain room into the back of the abode. There, past the simple wooden bed, the basic wooden chair and desk with its lonely metal rice bowl, peering from behind a sleek new washing machine, sat our monkey. Of the two, it was the washing machine that struck me as out of place, and I was tempted to ask him why a monk, living a strict life of self-denial, would have the modern convenience of a washing machine tucked secretly in the back of his home, but that would be something to ponder at another time.

My shaking fingers fumbled as I loaded a dart into the barrel of the gun. The beady black eyes from behind the washing machine watched suspiciously. Shooting at his defiant little face would likely kill him, and that would not have ingratiated me to my colleagues. I would need to wait until he darted off and try to hit his muscular backside, but I would only have one shot before he was gone again, and it would not be an easy one. The "foreign expert" had better not miss, I thought to myself.

We stared at each other—primate to primate, like a staring contest in a schoolyard. Tense seconds slipped by. I tried to ignore the bead of sweat stinging my right eye and the trickle down my back. Occasionally he would flinch, or raise his eyebrows, playing sadistically with my frayed nerves. But I was determined not to be outmaneuvered.

THWACK! The dart hit its mark on his hip and knocked him off balance as he dove for the drainage pipe. Maybe I had dialed the air pressure on the gun a little higher than necessary, but I was not taking chances. The dart had shot like a missile. The monkey shrieked, yanked out the offending barb, and hurled it angrily behind the washing machine. Intense eyes glared at me for a moment before they disappeared through the opening. The elder monk standing beside us was suddenly wide-eyed and fully awake. The young novice and I bowed, thanked him politely, and ran to find our monkey. There was no time for explanations.

The typical doses of anesthetic we used to dart monkeys would cause them to fall asleep in about ten minutes. In ten minutes, however, a frightened monkey can travel a long way over the rooftops, so we had doubled the dose, hoping for a quicker response. It did not take long before we caught up to our quarry. His four-legged sprint had slowed to a hurried walk, then a gentle stroll, and finally a drunken wobble, before he rested against a small guard house beside a huge red wooden gate. With great delight, I called Dr. Lin on the walkie-talkie.

"I didn't miss!" I blurted out. It was not very professional.

He arrived with the keeper and we waited as our patient's eyes grew heavy and his body slumped.

A group of old ladies walked by and noticed the resting monkey. Respectfully, they folded their hands and bowed. Apparently, the difference between holy temple monkeys worthy of worship, and escaping zoo rascals, was not obvious.

Propped up against the wall, it was hard to tell if he was just resting lazily or truly asleep, and I had no interest in risking my fingers picking up an angry, drunken monkey. Cautiously, we approached and gently prodded him in the side with the blow tube. He listed sideways and slumped into a comatose heap. I checked his heart and breathing and came to an unnerving realization. Our fuzzy little runaway was quickly passing sedation, and racing toward profound anesthesia and death. Fortunately, the whopping dose of sedative was reversible with an injection of antidote. In some animals, the reversal was almost immediate, which was great, but there, in the middle of the temple grounds, with no cage to put him in, it was a problem. There was nothing for it but to ferry him back to his own cage and then give the antidote, but time was not on our side, so we needed to hurry. The young keeper and I each took half a primate. He cradled the head and chest while I held the tummy and back end as we trotted through the temple grounds like two soldiers beating a hasty retreat. We jogged in step, bearing our limp patient in front of us, his arms and legs swinging lazily as we ran. *Left, right, left, right*, I thought to myself, trying to keep in step to avoid tripping and throwing an inebriated monkey at local tourists. We passed the temple gate and entered the zoo grounds. I tried to ignore the astonished gawking of the visitors and the screaming ache in my legs. We needed to cover about one more kilometre of ground before we reached our goal, and my mediocre fitness level was becoming evident.

Guests pointed, stared, and wondered, as we tromped along. Up the hill toward the aviary, past the unimpressed lions and tigers, around the corner at the giraffe enclosure, by the bored-looking elephants, and through the doors into the primate house. We reached our destination panting and heaving, and lay our limp furry burden on the floor.

My companion leaned against the wall, gasping for breath, as my tired fingers fumbled awkwardly with the syringe in my shirt pocket. The blood vessels of the monkey were now completely flat, and I would never find a vein in time, so I did the next best thing. I sunk the needle into his butt and depressed the plunger. With one last pat of his furry rump, we left the cage, closed it firmly and waited.

The battle between the life-saving antidote and fatal cardiovascular collapse had begun. Anxiously, we watched his chest. It rose and fell and stopped... for an alarmingly long time. *Breathe!* the voice in my head urged. *Breathe!* Then, after an agonizing wait, his chest rose again. I sighed with relief, and then wrung my hands as I waited for the next breath. After an exhausting half hour of helpless worrying, his breathing had stabilized and one eyelid quivered hesitantly as he

11

adjusted to the light. With a sigh of relief, I leaned against the concrete wall and watched my patient come around.

On my return to the vet hospital, the head keeper called me over.

"Hey," he said, "I just got a call on my cell-phone from a friend who is visiting the zoo today. He was frantic and yelling something about a foreigner running through the zoo. I tried to calm him and said, 'No, it's okay. He works for us.' But he just kept yelling, 'No, you don't understand. I'm serious! I am watching a foreign dude running through the zoo stealing one of your monkeys. Catch him before he gets away!'"

The keeper grinned at me and giggled.

In the course of one hour, I had been a tracker, hunter, doctor, athlete, and thief. Jesus said that if we followed him, we would have life and have it in abundance. I had no idea how varied and abundant life as a zoo vet in China would turn out to be.

I am the gate; whoever enters through me will be saved. They will come in and go out, and find pasture. The thief comes only to steal and kill and destroy; I have come that they may have life, and have it to the full. I am the good shepherd. The good shepherd lays down his life for the sheep.
John 10:9-11

Many people think of the Christian life not in terms of abundance, excitement, and joy, but as a period of prohibitions, austerity, and tedium. Basically—give up fun and excitement in this life so that you can go to heaven after you die (and even heaven doesn't sound like much fun, with all the clouds and harps and stuff—it's just better than the other option).

But the picture Jesus paints is very different. A life of abundance—filled with deep joy, meaning, and fulfillment on earth, and then ever-increasing bliss for eternity. The warnings and gates he puts in place during this life are there to keep the thief (Satan) from stealing our hope, killing our joy, and destroying our peace.

Jesus does not promise a life of ease or luxury or smooth sailing. But he does promise that, like a good shepherd, he will protect and lead and that it will never be boring. And he is willing to stake his life on that promise—literally.

Lord Jesus, forgive us for not taking you at your word—that you have come to give us life... abundant life. Give us eyes to see you as the loving shepherd you are—and to heed your protective warnings and come into the fold when you call us—and to follow you out into the pastures when you lead. Don't let us wander away from you and give Satan the chance to steal the joy that we have in you. Keep us close to you. In your name we pray. Amen.

Getting the Job

We dropped face down on our hotel beds—fully clothed. Our kids, two crammed in one single bed and two on the floor on extra blankets, were already asleep, which was not surprising after thirty-six hours of travel across twelve time zones.

"I'm beat!" I mumbled into the pillow.

We rolled over, used the last of our strength to pull off our street clothes, and tucked under the blankets. We had landed in central China after months of preparation and had overcome significant hurdles, but now, staring at the ceiling in our hotel room, we were wondering what we had gotten ourselves into.

"Go to the land where I am sending you. There I will show you what you need to do," God had said many months before. "Be strong and courageous," he had said. "Behold, I am with you always," he had said. And yet, having arrived in this strange place, we felt alone. We had spent the four previous years in Taiwan, teaching English and learning Mandarin, but it had been God's clear direction, confirmed in multiple ways, that pushed us to move to Mainland China. And now, we had landed deep in the heart of the "Middle Kingdom," at the foot of the Himalayas, in a moderately sized city of twelve million.

After many hours of travel with four young children, we yearned to fall into bed in our wonderful new home. The landlord had assured us it would be clean and ready for us the night we arrived, a promise I clung to with desperation as we touched down. We stumbled off the plane, gathered our twelve suitcases, multiple carry-ons, backpacks, and the extra wheelchair, and dragged it all to the van that was waiting to take us to our new home. The kids, bleary-eyed and grumpy, stared out the windows as the city lights drifted by. The finish line of our journey was in sight—and I couldn't wait.

We arrived well after dark, and I wearily swung open the door, ready to fall into bed. Dust, dirt, and an assortment of dead cockroaches carpeted the hall. It was completely deflating! Michelle rolled her eyes and our kids whined, so we did the only reasonable thing we could, and checked into a hotel for the night. Three days later, we finally moved in, the last step in a process that had started when I had left Michelle and the kids for one week to scout out China.

God had clearly called us so, six months earlier, I had taken that first step of obedience. I had to find a suitable job that would provide us with a work visa, find accommodations for our family of six, and do it all in less than one week. Such an assignment in Canada would have been challenging, but in China, with no leads or contacts for work, in a land where housing was built for families with only one child, it seemed impossible.

I landed and met Jack, my portly American friend. He was a big man in his early sixties, solid in character, with a calm resourcefulness about him. I had met him a year earlier, and he had suggested this city as a suitable location for our family. His gentle manner, broad smile, and placid nature hid a purposeful spirit, and I was glad to have him by my side.

We started by going to the visa office.

In order to register as a vet in China, I was told, I would need to open a veterinary hospital, hire staff, furnish the facility and open it for business. Then, *maybe*, they would consider giving me a work visa. It was more of an investment than I was willing to make for "maybe," and I was not the driven, entrepreneurial type. The next best option was to look for a veterinary clinic that might go out on a limb and hire a foreigner.

Walking back from the visa office, we passed a dog-grooming parlor next to our hotel. It was a small salon, with one bathtub and two metal grooming tables visible behind the storefront window, but it was clean, had a pink neon sign above the door, and represented one of the new start-up businesses that the opening Chinese economy was encouraging.

We stepped through the door, and I introduced myself. The salon owner, a bright young man in his late twenties with slicked-back hair, greeted us in English.

"I used to working for Coca-Cola," he beamed. "So I can speak English!"

He talked about the quality of the shampoos he used, pointed out the features of the grooming tables, and introduced us to his staff. He shared about the chain of pet salons he was opening and his hopes for expansion, pointing out his business acumen along the way. Once he was satisfied that he had done himself and his business justice, he circled back to inquire about the reason for our visit.

"I can no give you job," he said with a disappointed frown, pondering for a moment before his eyes brightened. "But I know best animal doctor in my city! Come, I give you his address."

He smiled confidently, scribbled an address on a scrap of paper, and handed it to Jack.

We left the young entrepreneur at the door of his shop, beaming and waving to his new foreign friends. It was a start.

The next morning, we walked to meet the esteemed veterinarian, Dr. Guo, at the Loving Heart Veterinary Hospital to see about the possibility of getting a job. Bundled up to fend off the morning frost, we stepped onto the street and were immediately swept down the sidewalk with the rivers of people. We drifted along in the current of humanity for a while, making a few turns here and there, and arrived at the clinic. It looked clean and professional—but quite different from what I was used to.

Stepping through the glass door, we entered a large open room. There were two doors at the far end. One led to a tiny surgery, the other to Dr. Guo's office. The rest of the hospital, reception desk, kennels, waiting area, exam tables, treatment area, IV stands, microscope, and pharmacy were all contained in the main room. Four clean stainless steel exam tables lined the bare white wall on one side. Two of them held sad-looking puppies strapped down by all four legs. A nurse was attending to one of them, adjusting an IV line. A row of cube kennels on the opposite wall held an assortment of patients barking out their complaints. Little coloured bottles of medicine on the steel shelf above the small reception desk made up the pharmacy. The waiting area comprised a set of four brightly coloured plastic stools that lined the glass wall facing the street. The red one was occupied by a somber-looking gentleman. His sad eyes focused on the sad puppy on the table. It was all a bit different, but the smell of disinfectant and dogs felt like home. A pleasant receptionist in a tidy uniform hurried to the door to meet us as we entered and ushered us into Dr. Guo's office.

The doctor, a man in his forties dressed in a crisp white lab coat, was sitting behind his large wooden desk, yelling at the person on the other end of the phone and waving us in with his free hand. Evidently, he was a busy man. We sat down and waited. He listened to the man on the phone, leaned back in his chair, and bit his lower lip. Then he rolled his eyes, hurled a final slur at the man on the other end, crashed the receiver down, and wiped his brow.

Having composed himself, he turned to us with a broad smile, stood up, and held out his hand. Dr. Guo was a distinguished veterinarian in his city, had travelled overseas, and spoke excellent English. He was pleased to meet a colleague from abroad and listened carefully as I lay out my proposal. I would work for local wages, did not expect special treatment, and tried my best to explain how hiring a foreigner would be good for his business. He watched me intently, nodded to let me know he understood, but seemed completely unconvinced.

As we talked, clients came in, pushed past the receptionist, and barged into the office, leaning onto the desk as they presented their concerns. Dr. Guo had little choice but to hear them out. I sat back and listened to their conversations. I understood very little, so I leaned in. *It must be this old lady's accent,* I thought. However, as clients came and went, I came to the unnerving realization that I understood almost nothing. I had spent four years studying Mandarin in Taiwan, but I could barely make out what they were saying. The local dialect, though related to Mandarin, was quite different, and I was not picking up very much.

An elderly gentleman arrived, anxiously petting the quivering bundle of brown curls in his arms, and nervously glancing back at a woman scowling in the waiting area. He mumbled something about bad medicine. Dr. Guo looked at me and explained. The owner had attempted to save money by vaccinating his own dog using a dubious concoction from an unscrupulous pet store salesman—resulting in a large open wound on the back of his wife's beloved poodle. She was sitting in the waiting room, arms crossed and glaring. Dr. Guo tended to the trembling poodle, reassured the owner, and passed the dog back to his scowling wife. Then he turned back to me.

"I don't think local owners will trust a foreigner," he said. "My clinic is small, and I don't feel right hiring someone as educated as you."

Dr. Guo had been abroad and knew that veterinary education overseas was well ahead of his own land.

"I'm quite content with whatever salary you feel is fair," I said.

He shook his head slowly and sank into silence as he leaned back in his chair, searching the office walls for insight.

Coming up empty, he turned back to me.

"Let's meet again this evening," he said. "Maybe I can come up with something for you. There's a great little tea house around the corner where we can meet. Here is the address."

He scrawled a name and address on a slip of paper and slid it over the desk.

We stepped back onto the street, dodged a careening bicycle, and wandered back through the sea of people in silence.

Rounding a corner toward our hotel, we noticed a noodle vendor, veiled behind the cloud of steam billowing from his pot. Around his little wheeled cart, customers on plastic stools, seated at tiny folding tables and hunkered over their bowls were slurping up their lunch. It was too inviting a scene to pass up and our deflated spirits could use refreshing. I offered to buy Jack lunch.

"La Bu La [Spicy or not]?" the noodle man asked.

"La!" Jack said confidently.

The noodle man smiled delightedly at Jack, looked at me, and raised an eyebrow.

"La!" I said, not wanting to appear weak.

Two large bowls of noodles arrived at our table, swimming in an angry-looking red sauce. Jack dug in, happily scooping up large mouthfuls and munching contentedly. I picked up a few strands, placed them gingerly in my mouth, and chewed thoughtfully.

A scorching numbness attacked my mouth. My eyes teared, sweat beaded on my forehead, and my rear end puckered in fearful anticipation of the future. I searched in vain for a cool drink to douse the flames. There were no drinks. The angry broth was the beverage that came with lunch. It was my first introduction to local cuisine, and it took several minutes for the flames to subside and my mouth to recover. I was building up the courage to take a second bite when Jack pushed back his empty bowl and patted his tummy contentedly. It was not his first rodeo.

After a recuperating nap and an evening meal of plain white rice, we made our way to the tea shop. We ducked through the door and paused, letting our eyes adjust to the large, dimly lit room and the smoky haze. Veiled clusters of men lounged on oversized chairs, sipping tea, puffing on cigarettes, and spitting empty sunflower shells onto the floor. The aging décor gave it a well-worn appeal. The little groups grew silent and stared as we passed by on our way to the table where our host was waiting. The broad rattan chairs groaned as we sank into them—especially Jack's. A waitress sauntered over and filled three tall glasses with green tea.

"This is *Zhu Ye Qing*," Dr. Guo said as he pointed to the little green spikes that rose and sank lazily in the glass. "It's a very famous tea in our city." He sat back and popped a sunflower seed into his mouth.

"I apologize once again that I cannot offer you a job," he said, ejecting the empty shell, "but I have a suggestion. Have you ever considered wildlife medicine?"

"Not really," I said. "I have fairly broad experience as far as vets go, and have done both pet and farm work, but wildlife would be new to me."

"That doesn't matter," he said, waving his hand. "My good friend is the director of the zoo. Shall I call him?"

My mind reeled. What did I know about lions, pandas, and monkeys? But God had led this far. Who was I to refuse? I looked at Jack, and then the good doctor—and nodded.

The next morning, the zoo called to invite me for an interview and stunningly, by lunchtime, I had a job. I would be a staff veterinarian at the third largest zoo in the country and was offered a two-year contract and a generous (by local standards) wage. Gratefully I shook the hand of the man who would be my new boss. I spent the rest of the afternoon wandering through the zoo with Jack, trying to grasp that the elephants, pandas, and apes would be my patients and that I would get to know them, not just as random wildlife, but as individuals, with all their unique personalities.

That evening I lay in bed trying to absorb the day's events and the impact they would have on my family. Coincidences happen, and I don't attribute every available parking space to divine intervention, but as I lay awake in bed that evening, amazed at God's provision, I marveled.

"In three days, you took us, foreign strangers in a city of twelve million, to a random pet salon, whose owner knew the best vet clinic in the city, who led us to a position *at a zoo*, which will give us a visa *and* is one of the most fascinating jobs on earth. Really, what could be more interesting than being an animal doctor at a zoo in China?"

I smiled to myself and snuggled under the covers. By the end of that week, I not only had a job, but had miraculously found a home, in our price range and large enough to accommodate our whole family.

I am showing you who I am and how I can guide you, God seemed to whisper as I started to drift. *But for me to keep doing that you will need to keep stepping out in faith, even if you have nothing to lean on but me. So be strong and courageous. This land of spice and tea and pandas, this is where I am sending you. But don't worry, I'll be with you every step of the way.*

Be strong and very courageous. Be careful to obey all the law my servant Moses gave you; do not turn from it to the right or to the left, that you may be successful wherever you go. Keep this Book of the Law always on your lips; meditate on it day and night, so that you may be careful to do everything written in it. Then you will be prosperous and successful. Have I not commanded you? Be strong and courageous. Do not be afraid; do not be discouraged, for the Lord your God will be with you wherever you go. Joshua 1:7-9

———— ◈ ————

Sometimes God asks us to venture into the unknown. To do something, or go somewhere, that is new and scary. But he never sends us alone or unprepared.

First, God promises to "be with you wherever you go." (Joshua 1:9) and "I am with you always." (Matthew 28:20) Think about that! The Creator of the whole universe will never leave your side, no matter where you wander, or where you end up.

Second, he gives us the rulebook for success, the blueprint for victory in life, the rubric for a life filled with his presence—his law—the Bible. Life may not always be easy (just ask Joshua a year or two after he crossed the Jordan), but it will be successful in the eyes of the only one whose opinion really matters—God, who promises to be with us every step of the way.

———— ◈ ————

Heavenly Father, keep us close to you. Cause us to hunger for your word and not turn from it. As you lead us into the unknown, remind us daily that you walk with us, even if the path leads through deep valleys. Fill us with your Spirit, that we may be strong and courageous. Drive out any fear of the unknown because we know that you—the almighty King—walk with us. Lord that is such a comfort. Help us to point others to you as they witness our calm faith, trusting you to lead us through life. Amen

23

Settling In

Two taxis, crammed with our family, the wheelchair, and our mountain of luggage arrived at our new home.

"Oh, you are here? I didn't know if you would come," the landlady said when we had called her from the hotel to express our concern about the grimy house. She apologized profusely, arranged for a crew of cleaning ladies to sweep out the dust and roaches, and then, in good Chinese fashion, offered to make amends.

"I'll take you shopping for furniture and pay for the children's beds," she offered generously, making up for the dirty house debacle, and then nonchalantly added, "and anyway, you seem like nice people and unlikely to take me to court."

I looked at Michelle's raised eyebrows. Take her to court? Because the floors were not swept? Where did that come from?

"My friend, who used to live in America, told me that foreigners like to sue people and that I should be careful renting to you," she explained sheepishly, smiling at James, our youngest, who was toddling around the living room. I was pleased that we were making a more likeable impression than she had expected and assured her we had no interest in suing anyone.

Over the course of the next few days, we travelled our city, piling our kids in and out of taxis as we shopped for food, household goods, and fixtures. Six "tall-nose" foreigners pouring out of a taxi always drew a crowd, but shopkeepers seemed very pleased to see us, and we soon discovered why.

As foreigners, we were seen as wealthy (which, compared to the average citizen, was true) and that we were too naïve to know what things ought to cost (also true). For these reasons, the prices offered to us were at times "normal" (there was a little room to bargain) and at times, a "double-price-foreigner-special." Early on we were caught out a few times and paid considerably more than we should have for a lamp, desk, or carpet, but after awhile we became wise to the tactic and learned how and when to bargain—vigorously, and every time. This was a challenge for us because, as polite Canadians, we were culturally wired to avoid confrontation, but we did our best to adjust. Making friends with the fruit vendor at the wet market down the road helped. She was a jolly lady, as wide as she was tall, with a bubbly laugh and a big smile, who always came out from behind her mounds of apples and oranges to hug the kids. Her stand was a welcome haven where we could lay aside our bargaining weapons.

Big-ticket items like a sofa or washing machine were negotiated differently. First, there was the expected haggling over price, from the five-thousand yuan sticker price to the more reasonable two thousand that the item was actually worth. Then came the negotiations over down payment and delivery. We learned quickly that paying the full amount prior to delivery was risky. Items could come late, or damaged, or in the wrong colour, or possibly not at all, and there was little recourse if payment had already been made. The landlady taught us to pay a minimal down payment and make up the difference on delivery.

This protected our pocketbooks but presented a new challenge: deliveries.

Items rarely arrived on the day they were promised, and the drivers, burly young men from the surrounding countryside, only spoke the local dialect, which was hard to understand in person, and nearly impossible over the phone.

"Yah bot a sofaa!" the voice on the phone would say.

"Oh, I'm sorry. I'm a foreigner. I did not understand. Can you say that again, please?"

There was a pause and a sigh, and then they would yell, "YAH BOT A SOFAAA!" assuming that yelling the same thing louder would help. It didn't.

"I'm sorry. I only speak Mandarin. I don't speak Sichuan dialect. I'm still not quite getting it," we would say embarrassingly. "May I ask please, who are you? What did we buy?"

"WE R AHT DA GAIT! OPUN UP!"

It was not until the surly men found their way to our door and started to unload that we sheepishly figured out what was being delivered.

These deliveries tested our patience and battered our egos and were especially unnerving for Michelle, who by nature tried to make people happy. For Michelle, every grouchy delivery let her know she had not succeeded and deepened her sense of failure at reaching these people whom we wanted to befriend.

About a week later I had to run an errand in the nearby town.

"I won't be long," I had assured Michelle, "and we are not expecting the washing machine until tomorrow, so you should be fine."

Luke, our eight-year-old, joined me for the adventure as we hopped into a three-wheeled bicycle taxi outside our gate. The shirtless little driver peddled and puffed in the sweltering heat, sweat dripping down his back. I tried not to feel guilty sitting on the shaded, cushioned seat behind him and comforted myself with the thought that I was providing him with income to feed his family. We did not haggle over his price.

On the way back, sitting behind another panting taxi man, a sinister idea snuck into my mind. It was one of those impish notions that seems ingenious at the time, but utterly foolish in hindsight.

"How about if I call mom and pretend I am a delivery driver?" I asked Luke with a playful grin.

"Do it, Dad. Do it!" he giggled and bounced up and down in his seat.

"Pretend you don't speak Mandarin and call her. Make yourself sound like a Sichuan local. It'll be soooo funny!"

I should have known not to trust the gleeful encouragement of an eight-year-old, but I flipped open my new cell phone and dialed.

"Wei, Hello," Michelle answered politely, using both the English and local greeting.

"HEYY!" I bellowed into the phone in what I hoped was a good impression of a local delivery driver. "EEES DA WAHSHING MACHEEN!"

There was stunned silence on the other end. Then hesitantly, "I'm so very sorry. I didn't quite catch that. Would you kindly repeat it?"

"WAA? YOU NO SPEEK? WAASHING MACHEEN DEIVERY!"

"I apologize. I'm afraid I don't speak the local dialect. Could you say that again slowly please?" she said, her strained voice quivering.

I admired her effort to remain polite and composed.

"OPEHN UP! WE AHR HEEER!" I hollered, much to Luke's delight.

"Please..." Her voice was now shaking. "I don't understand. My husband is not home. What did we buy?"

I could no longer restrain myself.

"It's okay, honey. It's me!" I said, waiting for a sigh of relief and a hearty laugh on the other end. What I got was silence and then a dial tone.

I looked at Luke with shock as I realized what I had done. I had danced on my poor wife's last unfrayed nerve.

Dialing frantically, I waited for her to pick up. Nothing. Maybe she had to tend to one of the kids I tried to tell myself. I hung up and dialed again, this time letting it ring for an embarrassingly long time. Nothing.

Anxiously I stared at Luke, who was realizing the gravity of the situation. It seemed funny at the time, but Dad was in trouble now!

"How about bringing home some flowers?" he suggested, wrestling with his guilt as an accomplice and trying to help his frantic father.

"Yes, good idea," I stammered and advised the peddling bike driver to pull into the open market near our home. The flower vendor was thrilled. Guilty-looking husbands make for an easy sale.

Running up the stairs, a fresh bouquet of roses in hand, I found Michelle in the kitchen with her hands in a sink full of dirty dishes.

"I'm so, soooo sorry," I said, hiding myself behind the flowers.

"Not funny. Not funny *at all*," she said, sniffing back a tear and chucking cutlery into the drying rack with unnecessary violence.

"Daddy bought you these," Luke said from behind me, pointing to the flowers.

Michelle turned and looked thoughtfully at the bouquet, her sheepish husband, and her son. Her scowl softened, and the little crease in the corner of her mouth hinted that she was fighting the urge to smile. She was still upset, but it *was* kind of funny! Hesitantly, I approached her and gently rested my hand on her shoulder. She didn't pull away.

"I'm still mad you know," she said, but her eyes were softening.

"Oh, I understand, my dear. It was not a nice trick to play on you. And I really am very sorry to have stressed you like that. Please forgive me," I said.

She put her arm around Luke, who was now hugging her waist.

"We love you mom," he mumbled softly into her apron.

"I know, dear," she said and smiled. "I love you too."

Receiving grace and forgiveness, even when we *knowingly* do foolish things, is incredibly liberating. God wants us to enjoy that freedom, and then pass that joy along, reflecting God's grace to those around us.

Luke, still worried and hugging Michelle tightly, looked up at his mother. Silently Michelle dried her hands with the dish towel and hugged him back. She was setting a great example.

*Be kind and compassionate to one another, forgiving each other,
just as in Christ God forgave you. Ephesians 4:32*

⸺◦⸺

It's funny about forgiveness. We mess up all the time. So when it comes
to forgiveness, we know we need it, we ask for it, we kind of expect it,
and sometimes even convince ourselves that we've earned it.

But when others offend *us*, we weigh their sin in our hands, trying
to decide if they deserve our forgiveness. Jesus leaves us no such option.
He forgave us a mountain of sin (10,000 talents worth in his parable
of the unforgiving servant), and he expects us to forgive those who sin
against us—to be kind, and compassionate, even when we have been
hurt or offended.

Unforgiven sin can be a terrible snare—for the offended. It can
bind us in chains of bitterness and anger. Christ offers us freedom. Not
only from our own sins, but also from the bondage of holding other
people's sins against them. We have been forgiven—which gives us the
ability to forgive.

⸺◦⸺

*Lord Jesus, when we consider your love for us, and how far you were
willing to go to win us back, and then realize that you freely offer that
forgiveness to us—we are amazed. Forgive us Lord, for thinking that we
deserve your love and forgiveness. We don't. It's purely a display of your
grace. And Lord, forgive us for thinking that we have the right to decide
if others deserve our forgiveness. Help us to remember that if you forgave
us, we need to forgive others. But sometimes we find it hard to forgive. So
we need you to help us, cause us even, to do so. Fill us with your love until
it bursts through our resentment and anger, and floods those who have
offended us. Animate our beings with your love. Cause us to be agents of
your grace and forgiveness, so that others can know what it feels like to be
forgiven and loved. For your glory's sake we pray. Amen*

First Impressions

Michelle saw me hold my queasy stomach and gave me a long, tight hug before I walked out the door to get in the taxi for my first day of work.

"You got this, babe," she had said encouragingly. But I was not so sure.

The initial excitement about working at a zoo was being smothered by my shocking lack of knowledge of exotic animal medicine. I had worked on farms and with pets, and treated a Vietnamese pot-bellied pig on one occasion, but I knew virtually nothing about elephants or vipers or pandas. Back home, exotic animal medicine was a full-fledged specialty. Die-hard enthusiasts would subject themselves to years of study *after* graduating from many long years in vet school, and then gleefully uproot their lives and move anywhere for a chance to work at a zoo. I had been hired by my new boss as the "foreign expert," and I feared my lack of expertise would quickly make him regret that decision.

The taxi pulled up to the zoo and a uniformed gate man peered inquiringly into the window of the cab.

"I'm here for work," I said through the open back window of the taxi.

He raised one eyebrow and looked into the back seat suspiciously. Foreigners don't work at Chinese zoos, they just visit them, and he was wondering if I was one of those crafty ones who was trying to avoid the two-dollar entrance fee. His eyes studied me as he reached behind him to pull a walkie-talkie from the table in his booth to make inquiries. Then, satisfied that I was not a scammer but still watching me with squinting eyes, he reached over to lift the gate.

We pulled into the vet department parking lot. I thanked the driver, stepped out of the cab, and took several deep breaths. I was about to sink or swim—to prove my worth to the zoo or be sent packing. I closed my eyes, asked for enough wisdom not to mess it up too badly, and stepped into my new career as an exotic animal doctor.

The veterinary hospital was a square concrete building, slightly darker than the slate grey clouds overhead. I stepped over the steel threshold and through the heavy security door. The tired walls of the dark hallway had seen better days, and the terrazzo floor was worn from years of scurrying feet. Plain steel doors opened to the offices off the main corridor. Dr. Li, the vivacious department head, was wandering down the hall to greet me. Her bright smile and calm manner immediately put me at ease. She was slender and quite tall by local standards, accentuated by her high-heeled shoes. In fact, she seemed far too elegantly dressed for veterinary work.

"Welcome, Dr. Paul. We are *so* pleased that you are here," she said, shaking my hand and smiling. "Let me introduce you to the team."

Eager faces appeared from office doorways and introduced themselves. It would take a while to figure out all the names, titles, and roles, but I was touched by the warm reception and genuine sense of excitement at my arrival. I hoped their enthusiasm would last.

Next, I was ushered down the hall, not to my office, but to the bathrooms. In contrast to the bare concrete of the hall, the privy walls were decked in shiny white tile. The sink was pristine and the clean wooden doors to the toilets hung straight and even.

"We had it redone just for you!" Dr. Li beamed.

I looked around in humbled amazement. The whole bathroom, tile floor to painted ceiling, had been renovated in anticipation of my arrival. The director of the zoo had deemed the old bathroom not suitable for a foreign guest and had ordered it to be completely redone.

"That was so very kind of you. Thank you so much," I said, putting my hand to my chest and smiling my best smile. Clearly, this was a big deal, and I wanted to make sure that my colleagues knew I recognized the gesture. I glanced into the stalls and noticed that none of them had a sit-down commode. All I saw were white ceramic squatty-potties.

These latrines are the norm in most of the world and are really more hygienic than the sit-down style we westerners are used to. You place both feet on the floor on either side of a ceramic bowl sunk into the ground, lower your pants and bend at the knees until your elbows rest on them, your backside hovering a few inches over the target. Nothing gets sat on, nothing gets touched. It is all very clean unless your aim (or depth perception or concentration or balance) is off—or if you are wearing slippery shoes. We westerners are not used to such calisthenics when using the potty and prefer to sit, but evidently the zoo felt I could make this cultural adjustment.

Next, I was told, Dr. Lin would take me on a quick tour of the zoo. He was a short, energetic young man, with a slight build, lively eyes, and a gravelly voice. His bright smile and lively banter immediately put me at ease.

"Come, I will show you our zoo," he said as he beamed up at me.

Dr. Lin would become a close friend and cultural confidant, guiding his inept foreign comrade through the finer points of local customs.

"Now," Dr. Lin said when we returned from the tour, "we are going out for lunch to celebrate your arrival."

The warm welcome had settled my uneasy stomach, and I was looking forward to experiencing more of the local cuisine. Dr. Lin and I were joined by several department heads and zoo leaders and walked out the main gate to a local restaurant. The arrival of the foreign vet was a good excuse to celebrate, and everyone seemed eager to enjoy a special meal, regardless of the reason.

We were led upstairs, away from the clamor of the main seating area, and entered a small private room with one large, round, linen-covered table.

"Please sit here," Director Tong said, as he gestured to the seat at the back of the table. Ancient custom dictated that this seat, farthest away from the door and facing it, was the safest if danger came crashing through the door, so it was reserved for honoured guests. I was expecting only friendly waitresses to come through the door but was flattered nonetheless.

In short order, waitresses arrived and loaded the table with local delicacies. Whole fish, cracking with crispy deep-fried skin; pale tofu cubes in a peppery scarlet sauce; fiery blackened ribs; steaming chicken soup with cabbage leaves; boiled peanuts on little plates; wafer-thin slices of pickled meat decorated with curls of pink radish and a bowl of white rice were on the table. These were accompanied by a bottle of red wine, cola, and a suspicious-looking little clear bottle with a red label.

Cheerful conversation flowed around me as we ate. Director Tong, the head of the zoo, sat beside me and regaled me with stories from his life, peppered with explanations of Chinese proverbs.

"So, what do you think of our zoo?" he asked, raising his eyebrows.

"It's great," I said, munching on a slice of pork. "Just lovely. I am so honoured that you would ask me to join your veterinary team. I already feel very much at home and look forward to working here for many years."

Director Tong smiled, nodded, and reached for the little bottle. Tipping a healthy portion of the clear liquid into two shot glasses he handed me one, took one for himself, stood, and, motioning for silence with his free hand said, "I would like to personally toast Dr. Paul and welcome him to our team at the zoo. Gan Bei [empty the glass]!"

He tipped his head back and emptied the glass.

"Do not be drunk with wine," the Good Book says. But it also says to honour those in authority over you, and being publicly toasted by the director was a high honour indeed. To refuse would have been very disrespectful. I was in a quandary. I had been warned of the local penchant to enjoy hard liquor. Not wanting to offend my new boss, especially in front of his employees, I had to reciprocate by emptying my glass. But emptying it repeatedly, so as not to offend the many other eager faces that were preparing to toast the new guy, would be an issue.

"I really don't drink," I said. "But in honour of you and this wonderful occasion, I will gladly 'Gan Bei.'"

I tipped my head back and tipped the fiery liquid down my throat. My eyes teared, I sputtered a little, and the guests cheered.

"I want to toast you too!" several cried.

Thankfully, my earnest plea to *not* drink was accepted, to a degree, and a compromise was offered. Toasting with water or cola just wouldn't do, so I would take tiny shots of red wine while my counterparts enjoyed the fire-water. It was a fair arrangement.

Returning to the zoo, Dr. Li, red-faced and a little wobbly on her high heels, ambled into her office, slumped her head down on her desk, and slept. I suspected that most of the others did the same.

I returned to my office, sat down at my desk, and opened my laptop. My veterinary books and equipment would not arrive for a while, and so, trying to bolster my meagre knowledge of exotic animals, I did some internet research on reptile disease. By four o'clock, Dr. Li had rested sufficiently to conduct a short meeting to discuss the medical issues of a baby hog deer, a diminutive species of deer, no bigger than a large dog.

"The little guy had difficulty breathing and has injured a hind leg during treatment," she said. "Tomorrow morning, we will take him to the human hospital for x-rays."

Dr. Lin leaned toward me and whispered, "We don't have an x-ray machine."

A lively discussion ensued regarding treatment options. I tried to understand the discussion in the local dialect, but it had been a long day, and the words just melted together. At one point, I was not sure if they were discussing an anus or a steel rod, a distinction that I would need to have cleared up. The discussion slowed, and they turned to me.

"What do you suggest, Paul?"

I stared at the expectant faces and quietly admitted, "To be honest, I have no idea what you just talked about." It was not an impressive start.

Patiently they explained the situation in Mandarin. It seemed most likely that the little creature had dislocated a hip joint, so I could suggest several courses of treatment, including the surgical removal of the head of the femur, leaving the body to create a false joint. It is a common procedure, which I had performed on dogs with hip dysplasia and had seen excellent results. Their shocked expressions, however, suggested that to them, simply cutting off half of the hip joint did not seem like a viable treatment option. Politely, they decided to see what the x-rays would show in the morning and go from there.

I returned home, my head swimming with experiences. Squatty potties, spicy food, seats of honour, avoiding drinking games while honouring superiors… There was much to get used to, and I prayed I would learn to understand the culture enough to avoid offending—or at least to avoid offending *too* much.

Paul said, "In everything set them an example by doing what is good,"
"I have become all things to all people so that by all possible means I
might save some."
Titus 2:7a and 1Cor. 9:22b

———◉———

God calls us to be his standard bearers—examples of his love to the hurting world around us. To live lives that are holy (set apart and different) and brimming with infectious joy and peace. To be so filled with his presence that people notice the difference and are drawn to it, and therefore to him.

But that requires us to be sensitive to others. To adjust our attitudes and actions to fit *their* culture and sense of proper behaviour, but never to the point of yielding to sin. It can be a delicate balance and requires God-given wisdom. It's easy to be a monk on a mountain-top, far removed from the temptations of the world. It's equally easy to give in to the sin around us, joining the world in its vices. Jesus calls us to live *in* the world (to relate to it, and connect with it, so that we can reach it with his love) but not be a product *of* the world, so that the world can see *him* through the contrasting example we set.

———◉———

Father, we need your wisdom to see others the way you see them. The insight not to offend them, even unintentionally, by our ignorance or stupidity. Give us the willingness to yield our own wants and desires to the needs of others, but never to the point of surrendering to sin. Cause our attitudes and actions to be so filled with the glow of your Spirit that those around us see the contrast and develop a yearning for the hope that we have in you, and then give us just the right words to share your love with them, and help us to do it with gentleness and respect. Amen

Of Drugs and Deer

My stomach had settled from the previous day's assault of anxiety, spicy food, and alcohol, and I was in much better spirits when I arrived for my second day. The gate man nodded and opened the gate with casual indifference. I was becoming part of his daily routine.

Walking into the main office, I lined up dutifully to sign in with the other zoo workers. Director Tong addressed me as I passed him on my way out.

"Good to see you are on time," he said. "I want you to know I treat all my employees the same, so if you are late, I will deduct it from your pay. No special treatment here."

He winked and grinned, but he was making a point, and I was oddly comforted knowing he saw me as part of the team.

Cornering the main office building, I made my way to where I thought the hog deer exhibit might be. The zoo was not large and was pleasantly laid out, with meandering paths that led visitors to the exhibits past carefully manicured bushes and colourful flower beds, through dark groves of swaying bamboo, and under parades of elegant gingko trees. It was a lush botanical oasis set, like a jewel, in the noisy concrete grime of the city. In small clearings, silent groups of retirees flowed through the slow rhythms of Tai-Chi, enjoying the cool of the morning to do their exercises.

I rounded the corner past the elk, and antelope, and found my way to the hog deer to search for the patient. As their name suggests, these stocky little forest dwellers are about the size of a pig—a very small one. Their chunky build, big black eyes, short dagger horns, and tan coat gave them a sense of determination and purpose, as if to make up for their small size with big attitude. I watched them tromp the well-worn paths of their enclosure and searched for a baby following its mother on three legs, or at least one with a limp, but each one marched by, a picture of health.

Very odd, I thought and made my way back to the vet office.

A young assistant watched me in the hall, going from office to empty office, looking for my colleagues.

"They have already left for the hospital," he said as I passed by.

I had been looking forward to the adventure of taking an exotic deer to a human hospital for x-rays and was a little dejected that I had missed out, so I shuffled to my desk and tried to distract myself with internet research.

The party returned mid-morning a bit glum, with films showing a broken femur, and news that the deer had died.

"We sedated him, but he vomited and choked, and now, he's dead," Dr. Lin said, pursing his lips.

Anesthesia carries risk, I thought, *but sedation for an x-ray should be pretty routine.*

"What do you use for sedation?" I asked.

"This," Dr. Lin mumbled as he handed me a small brown bottle.

I stared at the label. Xylazine was a fine sedative. One I had used many times, but it is incredibly potent, especially for ruminants like our little deer. The dose for sedation was minute, so our cat-sized baby deer would have needed just enough to fill the hollow of the needle and dosing would have been very tricky. I examined the bottle. Other than the name of the drug, all it said was 1-2 ml /100 kg. *How much of the drug is there in one ml I wondered?* I turned the bottle over and looked on the back, searching in vain for the concentration. *And 1-2 ml/ 100 kg for what? Cow? Pig? Elephant?*

"Oh, we don't know how strong it is," Dr. Lin said awkwardly. "We get this from the university and they don't tell us, only that one batch is more or less potent than the last one. So we have to guess a bit."

Sadly, that morning, they had guessed wrong.

I returned to my office and sat, staring at the computer screen. It was all a little disconcerting. Anesthesiologists don't like to guess—it's bad for business. I didn't want to guess either, especially if I was to be the foreign expert who was supposed to know stuff.

Later that morning Dr. Yang, the vet in charge of birds, reptiles, and neonates, knocked on my door frame. He was a polished middle-aged man with round glasses and a neatly pressed jacket. I thought his quiet voice and gentle manner were better suited to a library than to the controlled chaos of zoo medicine, but I liked him. He fidgeted awkwardly in the doorway.

"May I come in?" he asked softly.

"Of course," I said. "Please come in. Have a seat."

Dr. Yang sank into the chair and groaned softly.

"I feel so bad! I wish I had given less," he said. "It's often like this. We have to guess at doses. Too much and the animals die, too little and they struggle and hurt themselves. And when we get it wrong, the keepers are upset. It's not that we don't try..." His voice trailed off. "We have a hard time anesthetizing snakes too," he continued. "They wake up too fast."

This last bit of the conversation concerned me. The zoo had banded kraits, pit vipers, and cobras. The thought of one of those little danger-noodles waking up halfway through a rectal exam was unnerving. I asked if they had inhalant anesthetics that could be pumped into their cages as sticking a needle into an alert cobra left something to be desired.

"Oh yes," he said, brightening significantly. "I'll show you."

We walked back to the veterinary dispensary where the assistant produced a dark brown bottle of liquid for me to examine. The Chinese characters were unfamiliar but with the help of a dictionary we found the translation: di... diethyl... diethyl ether. *Ether?!?* I had heard of it, seen it used by nefarious villains in period movies, but had never used it myself, nor had it been mentioned in veterinary school. I thanked Dr. Yang and retreated to my office to search the web. I found it under "The history of anesthetics," which said: "Ether was one of the first anesthetics used. It is volatile, highly flammable and was used commonly to amputate limbs in field hospitals during the American civil war." It is not found in any modern veterinary formularies.

I was beginning to realize what a limited arsenal of drugs and equipment my colleagues had at their disposal. No x-rays, no inhalant anesthetics, limited and outdated veterinary books. Even hot water was not a luxury the veterinary hospital had the funds to install. These dedicated professionals were doing what they could with what they had available, which wasn't much. Veterinary work at the zoo would require some out-of-the-box thinking and creativity. It was daunting, but then, what is life without a bit of a challenge? And anyway, God never promised us a simple life, just that if we asked, he would provide us with the wisdom we need.

If any of you lacks wisdom, ask God, who gives generously to all without finding fault, and it will be given to you. But when you ask you should believe and not doubt. James 1:5-6a

———— ◉ ————

"I don't know what to do," we complain to God—and it's true. *We* don't know. But God—who loves us and knows our hearts, our situations, and the future and who embodies all knowledge and wisdom, *that* God—offers to share that wisdom with us. And not just a little taste, but a big heaping plateful of it. The omniscient God of eternity will make up for our lack of wisdom by opening the floodgates of his insight. James encourages us to ask for this wisdom in faith, without doubting. Why? Because God promises he will give it generously.

But he will not necessarily give it instantly. In Proverbs, God connects wisdom to humility (11:2), to self-control (13:3), rates it as more valuable than gold or jewels or anything we have (4:7), and ultimately ties it to the knowledge and fear of God. "Trust in the Lord with all your heart and lean not on your own understanding; in all your ways submit to him, and he will make your paths straight" (Proverbs 3:5-6). So when we don't know what to do, going to him for wisdom, and submitting to him in faith, is *the* place to start.

———— ◉ ————

Lord, so often we complain that we don't know what to do, and even blame you for not giving us clarity, but forget to come to you for insight and wisdom. Or we get mad at you for being slow to answer, instead of recognizing our own impatience. Forgive us for not seeking you and your wisdom first. Forgive us for not valuing it enough. Forgive us for our impatience when you don't answer on the timeline, or in the way we want. We are humbled that you are willing to lavish your wisdom on us and are amazed that you offer it freely, just waiting for us to come to you. Lord never let us take you, or your wisdom, for granted. Amen

Getting Around

I reached for the dashboard of the taxi and braced for impact. Michelle was in the back seat, wide-eyed and clutching our two-year-old on her lap with the other three squeezed in beside her. They were looking out the rear window or playing with the toys they had brought along for the ride, oblivious to the horrific accident that seemed inevitable. The red light and busy intersection we were speeding towards seemed of no consequence to the driver either. He was a stout little man, with a brush cut and a wrinkled shirt. His one pudgy hand fumbled for the mason jar of watery green tea wedged beside his seat. With the palm of his other hand, he spun the wheel to avoid a young man on a bicycle who, like my kids, seemed oblivious to his brush with death. We careened through the intersection, swerving to miss an old lady on a scooter, a shiny black Mercedes, and a honking bus, which roared by, inches from our bumper. Having made it to the other side, the driver let go of the steering wheel to unscrew the top of the mason jar. He tilted his head back and closed his eyes to have a long, satisfying drink, steering with his left knee, his right foot still pressing firmly on the accelerator. This was driving in China—an exercise in prayer and a workout for the adrenal glands. With every taxi ride, our hearts raced, our muscles tensed, and every sense was on high alert. The kids thought it was great fun, but for Michelle and I, it was exhausting.

The traffic of our city was organized bedlam. It was akin to bumper cars, but without all the annoying rules. Most of China's shiny new cars were driven by equally new drivers whose gleaming smiles hid their inability to steer and shift at the same time. Twenty years earlier, there had been no private cars in the country. Now the roads were clogged, and an extensive highway system ferried the gleaming new vehicles around. The variety of transportation was astounding. Gargantuan trucks piled high with teetering mountains of cabbage, diminutive vans with pocket-sized engines struggling to keep up, schools of bicycles flowing through openings in traffic, showy German sports autos, and the ubiquitous street sweepers (on foot with a broom) all mixed together in a happy free-for-all. The rules of the road were much like the rules of shipping. He who is bigger has the right of way. Buses and dump trucks stopped for no one and routinely barreled through red lights at full speed. Cars were next in the "right of way" order, followed by scooters, and then bicycles, which had very few rights. Pedestrians had no rights at all.

One of the favourite local traffic games was "Chicken." Chicken was played when two cars, five bicycles, eight pedestrians and a bus all dive for the same small opening in traffic. The winner was usually the one who closed his eyes and lunged ahead with the most gusto. Sometimes there are only losers.

Initially, as we were settling in, buying a car was low on the list of priorities. Beds, essential appliances, and food were more important and seeing as we didn't have local driver's licenses, we had no choice but to rely on taxis, which always provided for an exciting trip, even if the destination was mundane.

A destination that our kids found especially dull was their school, which was on the south end of the city. There had been several educational choices for our family, including homeschooling, local school, and international school. Homeschooling, we decided, was not for us. It worked well for some families, but we knew our personal limitations and knew we would not do well as both parent and teacher. Local schools, with their huge classes and rote memory approach to education did not seem ideal either, so we enrolled them in international school.

One day, the kids and I were returning from school by taxi as usual. Rachel, Luke, and Isaac were snug in the back seat, I was in the passenger seat, and Isaac's wheelchair was resting in the open trunk of the aging VW Jetta. As we cruised along the highway, drinking in the exotic scenery of our new home, a sudden jolt and shocking BANG had us gripping our seats and staring at the driver with wild-eyed fear.

"DADDDY!?!" came the wail from the back seat.

"Oh, it's nothing," the driver assured us and waved his hand.

I turned a fretful smile to the kids to comfort them, but they stared back at me, still gripping their seats.

Time passed, and our bodies relaxed.

Then the vehicle let out a second BANG and did a few short bunny hops! This time the driver also looked anxious and pulled over to the curb lane to slow down. By the third thunderous report, he stopped the car on the shoulder, got out, and looked underneath. Trucks hurtled past his rear end as he peered under the dying creature that was his car.

"I'm sure it's okay," he said hesitantly and got back in, easing the car down the road.

By the fourth explosion, the little car had enough and dropped assorted metal bits from the undercarriage. We ground to a halt and from that point on, all gears were neutral. The driver gave us an impish grin, and I had the opportunity to exercise by pushing an aging Chinese taxi along a busy motorway to the nearest off ramp. We were given a small discount on the ride and left alone to search for another cab.

That evening, Michelle and I decided we had had enough. Piling into cabs and arguing with drivers over where to put the wheelchair, haggling over prices, and now this. We needed our own vehicle.

We had owned our new van for only two days when someone hit us for the first time. It was a sunny Sunday morning, and we were on our way to the international church, glowing in the thrill of our new silver van. The other driver had a glowing smile on his face as well as he veered toward us, coming the wrong way up a one-way street. We made eye contact, and I realized he was not swerving or slowing down. My own smile melted away as I wondered what he was up to. I slowed and honked the horn for good measure, but he seemed determined to hit us and no amount of evasive driving on my part was going to change that. With a dull crunch, we came to a sudden stop.

We both pulled over to the curb and the driver, a thin gentleman in a thin coat got out and offered us twelve dollars for the dent and scrape he had caused. I had no reference for what such a repair might cost and told him I was new to the city, (which seemed painfully obvious once I said it), and that I would need to call the insurance company and the police. He rolled his eyes.

The policeman arrived, pulled up behind us, and surveyed the damage with bored disinterest. He suggested we agree on a price and leave it at that. I told him I was quite willing to do so but needed some reference for the cost of repairs.

"Can't get involved in price-setting for damages," he mumbled.

Another gentleman arrived. "Are you from my insurance company?" I inquired hopefully.

He grunted and bobbed his head, inspected the damage, and suggested twenty dollars. I agreed, was paid, and drove off to Sunday morning fellowship.

On the way my cell phone rang. It was my insurance company asking if their man had arrived. I assured them he had and thanked them for their prompt service.

"That must have been the other driver's insurance company," came the reply. "Our guy is still on his way!"

Later we realized that it was not anyone from *any* insurance company who made the damage assessment, but simply the other driver's local pal, but it didn't matter because, surprisingly, twenty dollars was enough to cover the damages. We arrived at fellowship a little late, but that was fine. We were safe and thanking God that the accident hadn't been worse. Getting around in China was going to be an adventure and not always easy, but as a friend once said, "It will either be a good time or a good story."

The Lord is good, a refuge in times of trouble.
He cares for those who trust in him.
Nahum 1:7.

———◈———

Nahum put it succinctly. First, *God is good.* Our circumstances may not always be good (accidents happen), but God remains who he is—he is good. The verse recognizes that even though God is good, there will be times of trouble. The two are not mutually exclusive. We live in a sin-diseased world so accidents, illness, loss, and tears will happen. But our God will still be good, and he asks us to trust him, even if we have an accident, lose our job, or death stalks our families. He asks us to see the bigger reality beyond our circumstances. To look past the obviously bad, and trust that he is still there, that he is still good, and that despite everything, he cares for us.

———◈———

Lord, when dark clouds roll in and trouble soaks our lives, help us not to lose sight of you. Be our refuge. Help us to trust in you and abide in you. Lord, may we constantly be amazed that you, the all-powerful God, know us, and care for us, and are offering to be our refuge. Thank you that our joy is ultimately determined by our relationship with you and not by our circumstances. Lord, remind us daily that you proved your love and goodness to us on the cross, and that our temporary suffering on this earth pales in comparison to an eternity with you. We love you too. Amen

Communication

I t was day four of my new job, and as I sank into my office chair, I congratulated myself on driving to work, parking, signing in, and making it to my desk—all without issues. I yearned for routine and predictability, so in the whirlwind of transition that had become my life, I was glad for this small step toward normalcy. My employers, however, felt I needed a change.

"Let's buy hay!" Dr. Lin called as he hurried past my door to refill his tea thermos for a road trip. Reluctantly, I hoisted myself out of my seat and made my way to the large white van waiting for us in the parking lot.

Buying hay is not much of a medical task, and seemed pretty simple, but in China inspecting hay before it was purchased was an undertaking that required a team of five: three vets, an animal husbandry specialist, and a driver.

Leaving the congested traffic of our city behind, we meandered our way into the countryside. Tall residential towers gave way to short grey apartment blocks, which got shorter and more sporadic, interspersed with small fields of rice, vegetables, and rapeseed. The lively conversation around me faded into the background as I rested my head against the window and drank in the scenery.

The farmland was fascinating. There were no expansive fields, wide vistas, or big tractors. Instead, ramshackle farmhouses huddled in a tight checkerboard of fields. Chickens pecked under lines of colourful laundry and ducks paddled about in small, murky ponds. Neat rows of dark green vegetables were offset by dry, ocher rice paddies, framed by raised earthen walkways. There were tiny clay barns with sagging tile roofs just big enough for a cow and a few pigs. It all made for fascinating variety. And everywhere there were people, tilling fields with hand tools, bicycling precariously along narrow raised paths, or lugging swaying mounds of cabbages in wicker baskets on their backs.

An hour later, we pulled into the dusty driveway of a farm near a little river. The farmer, a slender man in a loose-fitting shirt and loose-fitting pants, greeted us and led us down a dirt path past a chicken coop to a small pile of square bales, where our little entourage stopped. Everyone turned to me, expecting the foreign expert to do...something.

I knew nothing about crops, so I did the only thing I could think of—fake it. I knelt down and stared at the bale, shifting from side to side to view it from different angles. Then I teased out a few pieces and felt the hay, rolling it between my fingers. Next, I snapped a few strands in half and stared intently at the broken ends until finally, not able to think of anything else, I smelled them. I had no idea what I was doing, but as I inhaled, I closed my eyes, furrowed my brow, and tried to be convincing as an intimidating foreign crop expert, hoping to avoid any questions.

"What do you think?" the farmer asked the group hopefully.

I kept my eyes closed.

"It's too yellow," Dr. Lin started off.

"It's fine!" the farmer retorted, "It's supposed to be that colour. Hay is yellow!"

"Not *that* kind of yellow, and anyway, it's too tough."

"That is just the outside bales. The ones on the inside of the pile are very tender, see?"

"This one has mold on it."

"That one must have been closer to the river. The others are great."

The lively back and forth continued for an astounding fifteen minutes, after which, rather abruptly, Dr. Lin quietly hefted a bale into the back of the van and closed the door. Apparently, negotiations had ended, and so we all piled in and set off. Everyone seemed pleased with the results of the morning's endeavour. Clearly, I was missing a lot of the unspoken communicating going on.

Our next stop was a wildlife park. It was an expansive place, built in anticipation of rich city dwellers looking for adventure. The animals roamed freely in wide-fenced paddocks, creating an African safari experience. We were ushered into open-sided safari vans and set off, passing through the home of the giraffes, which ambled over to greet us, their enormous heads stooping down from on high allowing us to pet their velvety muzzles. They made no sound, but their intent was unmistakable—they wanted love.

Past the home of the gentle giants, we parked the open van and moved to a prison van with steel bars on the window openings and suspicious-looking claw marks in the paint. We took our seats and entered the habitat of the lions, tigers, bears, and cheetahs. As we wound our way through the paddock, a park employee opened a plastic bucket and started waving bits of raw meat through the bars of the windows with long metal tongs. Lions ambled over for treats. Some of the more athletic members of the pride clung to the bars on the side of the bus as they were being fed. It was riveting! Other meat-loving hunters made their way over, looking for goodies. One particularly impressive brown bear hooked his claws on the steel bars, rocking the bus from side to side and roaring for food, his hot breath warming my face as it blew past the yellow canine teeth inches from my face. Like the giraffes, it needed no interpretation. His message was quite clear. For him, it was snack time. For me, it was a lesson in controlled terror.

Back at the main entrance, shaken but intact, the wildlife park director invited us to lunch. It was a welcome opportunity to sit and allow my nerves to settle over a hot bowl of noodles. By early afternoon, we were back at the zoo.

"Time for a rest. It's been a busy morning," my colleagues said.

My adrenaline levels, however, had not returned to normal after the bear incident, so instead of resting, I busied myself with research.

After rest time, we walked to see the zoo's tallest patients.

We knocked on the door. A tall, lanky gentleman blinked in the daylight as he opened the door. Taller Chinese were rare, so it seemed oddly fitting that the giraffe keeper was tall. Even his manner was much like the animals in his care. He was shy, quiet, and kind.

He led us silently up a set of gloomy back stairs onto a bright, open second-story roof-top patio. I leaned on the fence beside the feed trough and watched as Haihai, the powerful bull giraffe, ambled over. He was an impressive specimen and seemed calmly aware that he was very tall, very strong, and very handsome. We met face to face, two stories off the ground, his huge dark eyes inspecting me as he leaned forward to touch my outstretched hand with his soft muzzle. He smelled like warm grass. His long blue tongue, thick as my forearm, wrapped itself around the handful of hay I held out to him and disappeared, taking the hay with it. He chewed slowly and methodically and then, having seen enough of the foreigner, ambled off again.

The keeper pointed out the female in the distance. She was the reason for the visit. The zoo very much wanted a baby giraffe and had invested their hopes in this graceful female. At six years of age, she was mature and very much the picture of a shy, elegant young lady. Her soft round tummy and slightly enlarged udder suggested pregnancy, but for now it was only an educated guess.

"Her blah-blah-blah has not changed yet," Dr. Lin explained.

I stared at him. My street Mandarin was passable, but my medical vocabulary still left a lot to be desired, which meant that the key parts of many sentences were a mystery to me, and I was left to guess what part of the animal it was that was swollen, injured, or missing.

"Sorry, what is it that hasn't changed?" I asked sheepishly.

Some awkward charades and sign language ensued, but Dr. Lin and I were making little progress. The tall, quiet, giraffe keeper, sensing my frustration and Dr. Lin's awkward stammering, broke in gently: "It's where the baby comes out."

Dr. Lin smiled hopefully, and I nodded. The keeper looked relieved, and we all climbed back to the ground floor a little more informed.

I had learned a lot about communication that day. Hay bartering showed me that cultural expectations are a key component of communication. The giraffes and bear at the wildlife park had taught me that meaning can be clearly conveyed without words, and the awkward exchange about lady parts reminded me that sometimes it is necessary to lay decorum aside and just say what you mean.

Be quick to listen, slow to speak, and slow to get angry. James 1:19
A word fitly spoken and in due season is like apples of gold in settings of silver. Proverbs 25:11
I tell you, on the day of judgement, people will give an account for every careless word they speak. Matthew 12:36

———— ◉ ————

Ever since sin entered the world, communicating with each other has been fraught with problems. We talk more than we ought, and listen less than we should—and therefore we rarely *hear* each other. God reminds us to be quick to listen, to slow down, and think before we speak and to be patient in our response, especially if it involves anger. He also points out that a well-chosen word—just *one word*—spoken at just the right moment, is rare and beautiful like exquisite jewelry. Words are powerful and God encourages us to choose our words wisely because one day we will need to explain every word we have said, even (and maybe especially) the ones we tossed about casually without much thought. God gave us the gift of words and language and wants us to use that gift to encourage and build up, share love and grace, and point to truth, so that others might see him.

———— ◉ ————

Jesus, teach us to communicate like you do. To not only listen well, but, like you did with Nicodemus and the Samaritan woman at the well, give us ears to hear the question, the heart, or the struggles behind the words. Help us to hear in others what you hear, and then show us how to respond with patience, love, grace, and truth. Help the attitude of our heart, expressed in our words and conversations, to always point toward you. And, as David said in the psalms, "Set a guard over my mouth, Lord; keep watch over the door of my lips," so that we use your gift of language as you intended—for the good of others, and for your glory. Amen.

Back to Basics

After the "great hay adventure," I was happy to be strolling through the zoo again. There was still much that was unfamiliar, so I needed to get better acquainted with the zoo and its residents if I was going to make any difference.

"Why don't you spend the day with Dr. Yang?" Director Li suggested during morning rounds. "He can show you his area of the zoo."

I liked Dr. Yang. He was the shy, quiet, cautious member of the team.

"Maybe... if you think it's okay... we could possibly try...," he would whisper during group discussions. His ideas were good, but he wasn't assertive enough to present them with confidence. I looked forward to time together learning about the feathered and scaly residents he was in charge of—as well as the babies. Everybody loves babies.

I followed him to the drug room and perused the shelves looking for English labels, while my colleague picked out an assortment of brown glass bottles and a few syringes and stuffed them in his suit pockets along with gauze squares and rubbing alcohol.

As we made our way along the winding paths, Dr. Yu quietly pointed out different birds and trees and shared their story in Chinese history. It seemed he spent a lot of time enjoying a good book but had few people with whom to share his knowledge. I was happy to be his audience.

We passed the reptile house and aviary and made our way to the petting zoo.

The petting zoo contained a small herd of goats, a Holstein heifer, a group of snuffling Vietnamese pot-bellied pigs, and a pool with two sea lions. It was a happy place where, for a small fee, visitors could buy small handfuls of yummies to feed the residents. Two little boys bought fish heads attached to a string and pole and were giggling as the sea lions came up to snatch their treat. Across the path, a group of kindergarteners squealed delightedly as goats munched the handfuls of hay they were holding through the fence. I wanted to join them, but Dr. Yang reminded me that we had work to do.

Our first patient was a sad-looking little nanny goat. One half of her udder was swollen and red. Mastitis—infection of the udder—was a constant concern for dairy cattle, so this, finally, was something that felt familiar. It was having its udder stripped out every two days and was being treated daily with penicillin injections.

"The solution to pollution is dilution," my veterinary professors had said. "Better to remove bacteria than just to treat them with antibiotics. So drain, wash, flush, scrape. Do everything you can to remove bacteria and then use antibiotics just to mop up what's left."

I knelt down beside the little goat, who was standing splay-legged to keep her thighs from touching her udder. Her dark expressive eyes looked back at me, hoping for relief. Gently I palpated her hot, swollen udder. Dr. Yang and the keeper watched expectantly, sure they were about to witness the curative magic of modern western veterinary medicine.

"Would it be possible to strip the infected milk out of the udder two or three times a day instead of just every two days?" I asked. "And is there a baby goat that we can put in with her to suck on the healthy half of the udder? That could help to keep the other side from becoming infected."

Dr. Yang looked thoughtfully at the goat, a bit disappointed at this basic suggestion. It was not the miraculous solution he was hoping for.

"Let's try it," he said to the keeper, whose deep sigh made it clear how he felt about my "expert advice" and the extra work it was adding to his day.

Attached to the petting zoo was the neonatal area for sick or abandoned zoo babies. We stepped through the entry and into the small concrete building.

"A Fei-Fei was born last night and is coming in," a keeper said as he rushed by with an arm full of towels.

What is a "Fei-Fei"? I wondered. At a zoo, it could be anything: tiny or huge, furry or scaly, adorable or vicious.

Through the dusty window, I could see two keepers trotting down the path. One of them cradled a newspaper bundle under his arm. He stepped into the building and lay his package on the table and peeled back the business section to uncover the small, sad, wrinkled face of a baby baboon. His mother had not cared for him well, holding him in a slaphappy sort of way, right-side up, up-side down, dragging by a back leg or just leaving him exposed on the concrete floor of the enclosure. The little guy was a pitiful sight. Wet fur had dried to his gaunt little body in ragged patches. His eyes were sunken and seemed beyond caring. But he still huddled his arms around him, hugging himself to ward off the cold. If his momma was not going to love him, at least he would try to love himself.

"Can I check him out?" I asked eagerly.

Dr. Yang seemed quite happy to let me step in so that he could watch the "great foreign expert" at work.

But the "great foreign expert" had never done a physical exam on a baboon.

Pretend it's a cat with opposable thumbs, I thought. *Start at the nose and work your way back.*

It was unlikely that the physical exam would provide a specific diagnosis (which would further disappoint my colleague), but it was a necessary step in the process, so I got to work.

I leaned over the little tyke, running my fingers over his gaunt frame as I ran through my mental checklist.

· Nose: normal—no discharge or bleeding.
· Eyes: sunken and dull—likely from dehydration, but no inflammation.
· Lips and cheeks: normal.

So far so good.

I opened the little mouth to check the gums, palate, and throat. It was my first baboon oral exam so I wasn't confident, but I, a fellow primate, had looked in my own mouth many times, and figured his should look similar.

It didn't. It all looked *very* wrong.

There was no tongue. In its place was a mangled mass of nondescript, dead muscle tissue, all the way to the back of his little throat. *Infection?* I wondered. *No, not enough time since birth for infection to take hold of his tongue to that degree. Cancer? No—too young. Nutritional? Nope. Trauma? Hmmm... possible.* I checked his lips, gums, and cheeks for evidence of abrasions or cuts that might point toward an injury. Nothing. Back to my list. *Autoimmune? Not likely. Congenital? Hmmm... yes. That seemed the most likely.*

Somehow the blood supply to the tongue must have been disrupted at a late stage of development and so instead of a dexterous little tongue, he had a ragged, mangled lump of flesh. I closed his mouth. The diagnosis was obvious, but I kept going with the exam.

It was part of the process, and I was demonstrating technique and method, not just looking for an answer. Lungs, heart, abdomen, pulse—everything else was normal. I removed the thermometer from his little backside to finish the exam and looked up at the eagerly expectant faces hovering over my shoulder.

Picking up the little baboon, I wrapped it in a towel and snuggled it against my chest, petting his fuzzy little head with my finger. He snuggled in, reached up to hold the button on my shirt, and closed his eyes.

"Well, what did you find?" Dr. Yang asked cautiously.

"It's not good news," I said, looking down at my patient. "He can't nurse because his tongue didn't develop normally. We can try tube feeding, but without a tongue, his chances are pretty slim."

Dr. Yang nodded slowly, took the baboon, passed a thin rubber tube through his nose into his stomach, filled his hungry little tummy with milk, and laid him in an old incubator. He looked lonely and miserable, his tiny body wrapped in a towel, vacant eyes staring at the dirty walls and scratched plastic window of his little chamber. The digital temperature readout on the rusty control panel flickered the temperature. Thirty-seven degrees. The old incubator couldn't replace the nurturing arms of a loving mother, but at least it was warm.

Back in my office I reflected on the morning. A complete history, physical exam, and record-keeping did not seem to be part of the routine at the zoo. However, doing them (and doing them well) would take time, effort, and practice. In diagnosis, fancy lab tests are just the final touch, used to confirm a suspected disease. It's the basics—the thorough, well-practiced history and physical exam—that make up ninety percent of a diagnosis.

We do the same with God. We forgo the basics (regular time in the word and prayer), which seem mundane and require time and perseverance, and look for new, flashy, instant ways to deepen our relationship with him. But there is no replacement for the basics.

Devote yourselves to prayer, being watchful and thankful.
Colossians 4:2
I meditate on your precepts and consider your ways. Psalm 119:15
I wait for the Lord, my whole being waits, and in his word I put my hope.
Psalm 130:5

———◉———

We don't like to slow down, or wait, or quietly meditate on Scripture. Old stalwarts like persistent prayer and regular Bible reading seem stodgy and inefficient. We like new and instant. So, we turn to podcasts guaranteed to uncover spiritual secrets, to special prayer formulas to hurry things along, or to an alternative approach to spiritual formation to catapult us to maturity, trying to avoid all that time sitting at God's feet.

But relationship (including our relationship with God) takes time and effort. It requires a deep devotion to the basics. Talking with him, meditating on his word, and spending lots of time in his presence. It is a lifelong pilgrimage, at a marathon pace. A long obedience in the same direction that leads to the ultimate reward—God himself.

———◉———

Heavenly Father, forgive us for looking for shortcuts to our relationship with you. For trying to find alternatives to spending time with you, because we value your gifts more than we value you. Lord, slow down our lives and teach us your ways. Give us a desire for your word and the resolve to read it daily. Make us diligent in prayer, and reignite in us the joy of sitting quietly at your feet. Lord, help us nurture these disciplines so that we might gain that incalculable treasure— a deep, abiding, eternal relationship with you. Amen

Hidden Bones

It was an exceptional day—a *sunny* day. In Chengdu, as the sweltering heat of summer gave way to autumn, the sun disappeared behind a curtain of slate grey clouds and was kept there until the spring. In the winter, we would see the sun once a month—maybe.

So, on this bright fall day, the lions were draped about their exhibits, eyes closed and snoozing. The storks and wading birds strutted happily, blinking in the brightness, and the busy squirrel monkeys frolicked in sun-dappled trees. The baby baboon was still with us and had a little more spirit, and the world seemed to be a happy place.

After our morning rounds, Dr. Yang and I joined the rest of the veterinary team at the primate exhibit. A black langur monkey was unwell.

In their prime, these are stunning animals with metre-long tails and gangly limbs. Their shiny black fur crests to a pointy mohawk on their heads, a feature accentuated by pure white streaks along both cheeks.

Sadly, our male, squatting in a dark corner of his enclosure, was not enjoying the sunshine. He was preoccupied with other concerns. The white streak on the right side of his face highlighted a swelling that ran from his mouth to his ear. His lips were too misshapen to close, and he was clearly in distress. However, an oral exam like we had performed on our little baboon was out of the question. His glaring eyes made it clear that even at a mere fourteen pounds and weakened by his illness, he would not tolerate shenanigans. Monkeys can be fierce, and I liked my fingers where they were, attached to my hand.

He sulked against the concrete wall and hardly flinched when the ketamine dart hit his leg. He stared at it for a while, wondering if it was worth the effort to pull it out, but he took too long deciding and slowly softened into a sleepy heap. Two of the keepers fetched him and laid him on the wooden crate that served as our exam table. He was sedated, but not fully asleep, so the keeper held his arms for good measure.

Back to basics, I told myself.

-Nose: some blood-tinged discharge from the right nostril.

-Eyes: swelling of the skin around the right eye

-Lips and cheeks: right side swollen.

I lifted his lips to inspect his mouth. Huge dagger-like incisor teeth guarded the entrance. Tucking my thumbs under his front teeth, I pried the jaws open. A putrid trickle of pus oozed over his swollen red gums and down his molars. Evidently, the poor guy had not opened his mouth in quite some time. I reached past his formidable incisors and wiggled a molar. It wobbled easily. I looked up at the others.

"There is a lot of infection here, so we need to extract some of these teeth," I said.

Dr. Li looked down at the sharp teeth and the smelly pus and smiled at me.

"Go ahead," he said.

I eased my fingers past the incisors to grab hold of one of the molars wobbling in the rotten gums and gave it a gentle tug. *Oral abscesses—nasty stuff,* I thought to myself as I pulled it out.

We gave instructions for soft food and oral antibiotics and returned to the office. The oral antibiotics were not ideal for the diet of his complex leaf-eating digestive system, but darting and injecting him twice a day was risky too. We were doing our best with our limited options.

It had started as a cheery day, but the sad state of our patient and a call just before lunch that the baboon baby had died dampened my mood. "Where there is livestock, there will be dead stock," an old farmer once told me, but illness and death still made me sad.

After lunch (macaroni casserole, much to the curiosity of my coworkers), Dr. Lin came to my office.

"Have you ever been on the roof?" he asked.

I needed a little cheering up, and such a splendid sunny day did warrant a trip to the roof of our three-story building. We climbed the dusty concrete stairs and stepped out onto the flat tile surface. Dirt, a few tufts of grass, and an enormous pile of crumbling, moss-covered elephant bones lay exposed in the afternoon sun.

"Where are these from?" I asked, wondering how elephant bones came to be on the roof.

"Those are from an elephant," Dr. Lin replied. "Bones of special animals are buried until the meat has decayed and then put on the roof to dry."

Unfortunately, the humid, cloudy weather of Chengdu did not lend itself to the drying out of bones. The elements had reduced these sturdy frames to a parchment consistency that flaked off thin crumbly layers when we moved them.

Further along the flat roof lay a rhino and giraffe skeleton. These were still in reasonable shape. I looked at the pile of rhino bones. The massive skull, thick femur, and heavy humerus all bore testament to the colossal creature they were designed to hold up. I knelt down, lifted one of the heavy bones, looked at the pile, and smiled. It had been a long time since I had put together a puzzle.

"What do you think?" I asked.

"Oh, we need an expert to come and do that. There are too many bones."

"Nonsense," I said. "There are only about two hundred bones, and we ought to know how they fit. After all, we are vets."

I picked up a vertebra and found its partner, fitting them together and laying them on the roof. Looking a little further, I found two more that matched. Dr. Lin found the next one in the set. Five were lined up, curving gently in order of size and shape. They begged to be reunited with their scattered friends. We searched for the rest among the moss and grasses of the roof and laid them out before us. It was not long before we had the entire backbone and bulky head of a rhino assembled. The neck bones were particularly impressive, built to hold up the massive head and ferocious impact that a rhino could deliver. With only the backbone and blocky head completed, it looked like the skeleton of an ugly dolphin. It needed legs to give it balance. The pelvis, back legs and front legs were heavy, but easy to find and place, though sadly, we were missing a humerus and one kneecap. Next came the ribs, lined up in order of size. That part was straightforward. Finally, we set to work on the challenging heap of cube-like toe and foot bones. Inspecting each piece, we laid them out as best we could.

"Cha bu duo [close enough]," Dr. Lin said as he placed the last of the foot bones. He stood back with his hands on his hips and smiled. The impressive bones lying before us in the sunshine were a marvel. Rugged enough to support two tons of Rhino racing at fifty kilometers an hour and able to withstand the earth-shattering collision when it hit.

I admired the bones. They were impressive examples of one of God's more rugged inventions. Bones are not static, like some boring internal scaffold. They are alive and active and constantly remodeling, so that every ten years we have an entirely new skeleton, all without interrupting daily life. Bones hold us up, keeping us from being a floppy pile of soft organs in a bag of skin on the ground. They also protect the most delicate organs, like our lungs and heart behind a cage of ribs and shield our pudding-like brain in the fortress of the skull. The outer, load-bearing core of each bone is composed of miraculously dense material that is both rigid enough to withstand tremendous stress (a human femur can hold up about six thousand pounds), but also elastic enough not to shatter on impact. Inside the robust outer layer lies a delicate latticework of bone which holds the marrow, the blood-producing factory of the body. In people, that marrow produces over ten billion new blood cells every hour!

I marveled at these normally hidden (but vital) body parts, lying exposed in the sunshine. Which made me think of how much of life is hidden, and how grateful I was that even these hidden (and often forgotten) bits of our lives are still graciously sustained by the Father.

It is he who reveals the profound and hidden things; he knows what is in the darkness, And the light dwells with him. Daniel 2:22
Do not be anxious about anything, but in every situation, by prayer and petition, with thanksgiving, present your requests to God.
Phil. 4:6

———◈———

One of the great comforts in our relationship with God is that he releases us from worry. He knows everything, and sustains everything. There is nothing that takes him by surprise, and nothing he doesn't have complete control over, and he loves us! That means we don't need to worry about all the things we can't control or see. If we have concerns, we can take them to him in prayer, because he knows all the things hidden in the darkness, and he controls them. So, we can leave it all at the foot of the throne and climb serenely onto the lap of the one who loves us, because *he* is the strength who holds us up.

———◈———

Heavenly Father, forgive us for worry. For not trusting that you are big enough, strong enough, or loving enough to handle our struggles. Lord, when we consider that you keep our organs working, our minds thinking, and our bodies upright, all without us spending a moment thinking about how to make it happen, we stand (forgive the pun) amazed. Thank you for the calm assurance that you know all things and control all things, and therefore we have nothing to fear—because you are God and you love us. And we love you too. Amen

Nasty Discoveries

Dr. Li looked down at her clipboard and traced the morning's job list with her finger.

"Dr. Paul, this morning you will follow Dr. Wu."

I leaned forward and grinned excitedly at Dr. Wu, who was leaning against a wall at the back of the room chewing on a toothpick.

Dr. Wu, the tall quiet vet on our team, did not smile back. He was the carnivore vet. The guy in charge of the big cats. The man who could meet strangers at a bar and say, "I take care of lions." As the keeper of the big cats, it seemed appropriate that he maintain a certain aura of cool disinterest, and having a chatty Canadian vet bouncing at his side was sure to cramp his style.

I put my hands in my pocket as we walked along the winding path, trying not to bounce, but it was hard. I was about to work on tigers and lions!

"That's our oldest male," he said, nodding casually to an enormous lion soundlessly pacing his exhibit on plate-sized paws as we walked by.

I tried not to stare.

"That's our female Bengal," he mumbled.

Two hundred and fifty stunning pounds of lithe power floated past the plate glass window of her enclosure.

He strolled on, hands in his pockets, and finally gestured to a sliding grey steel door at the rear of the leopard exhibit.

"We're in here," he said and stepped inside.

Dr. Wu nodded to a sullen keeper seated on a rickety rattan stool in the damp dark corridor behind the cages.

"Which one is he?" he asked.

The keeper nodded casually toward the door at the end of the hall but said nothing. It seemed that cool disinterest was the fashion among the big cat professionals.

I watched with rapt attention as Dr. Wu pulled out the fancy imported dart gun and loaded a syringe. Behind the bars, the muscles of a Chinese leopard rippled under his fur as he crouched in the far corner. He readied his claws, folded his ears back against his head, and tightened his lips to reveal his formidable teeth. A low growl completed the warning.

Dr. Wu set the pressure on the dial, leveled the barrel, and let fly through the bars of the cage. Slowly the tight muscles softened, the claws relaxed, and the lips smoothed as the vicious killer relaxed and became a fireside companion.

Cautiously, the keeper entered the enclosure with a large wooden board and prepared to move the big cat to a transport cage for shipment to another zoo. Sedating and relocating rare animals to prevent inbreeding turned out to be a frequent occurrence. For me however, it was new and exhilarating. But for the sake of my colleague, I muted my grinning as we walked back to the hospital.

"Unfortunately, the langur is not doing any better," Dr. Lin announced at the afternoon staff briefing. "Injecting him is getting difficult, and he is even refusing the children's antibiotics that we bought from a local pharmacy. And I was so sure he would like the grape-flavoured ones."

Eyebrows furrowed, heads were scratched, and a sullen gloom hung in the air as we searched our minds for options.

"If we don't know what to do, we will call a dentist to get their input," Director Li said resolutely and spun around on her high-heeled shoes to make the call.

Surely that is not necessary, I thought. *We should be able to figure this out.* But my silent protest remained silent, and a local dentist was called, and surprisingly, appeared at the hospital only a few minutes later.

We wandered back to the enclosure, a silent entourage. Dr. Lin and myself leading the way, followed by Director Li and a young lady dentist, her face still covered by her surgical mask and white lab coat from work. I imagined her human patient, still sitting in her dentist's chair, looking around and wondering what kind of critical emergency could leave him abandoned so suddenly.

Back at the enclosure, we tipped sedative into new dart syringes. The langur glared from the back of his concrete cage, but his body didn't tense. He made no attempt to run when he saw the blow tube, and when the dart hit, he did not scream or flee. He had lost his will to fight.

We stepped into the enclosure with our dentist in tow. The langur's limbs lay flaccid on the concrete, but despite his wilted state, the swelling pressing on his mandibular joint made it hard to pry his jaws open.

Dr. Lin and I held the open mouth of our patient into the light for the dentist to have a better look. She furrowed her brow, squinted her eyes, and shifted to get a better look.

"Looks like cancer to me," she said casually and stood up, brushing off her lab coat.

Of course! How stupid of me, I thought, as my pride took a heavy blow. The history fit perfectly. A wound that wouldn't heal, continued swelling, and infection despite antibiotics, an older patient—all signs that pointed to cancer, most likely squamous cell carcinoma. And I had missed it! I felt like a fool. The foreign "expert" should have known, but my mind quickly went back to our patient. More than his ego had taken a beating. He faced a malignant cancer that had already invaded half of his face and had most likely spread to other parts of his body. There was not much we could do. Radical surgery would not be an option, nor was chemotherapy. The only thing we could do was to allow him to live out the remainder of his days as peacefully as possible—and maybe give him some extra bananas.

I walked back to the hospital in silence, saddened at the inevitable fate of our langur, and deep in thought about cancer.

Cancer is vicious and horrible. It is not a minor mistake or feeling a bit under the weather. It is a deadly disease that invades every part of the body. And like sin, it kills—unless you can find a cure.

If we claim to be without sin, we deceive ourselves and the truth is not in us. If we confess our sins, he is faithful and just and will forgive us our sins and purify us from all unrighteousness. 1 John 1:8.9

———◆———

Like an early cancer, the root of most sins seems minor and easy to ignore. But as it grows, sin, like a cancer, starts to invade other parts of life. That slight excess of wine starts to affect the family; small lies balloon, with unintended consequences; and that slight envy grows into soul-draining bitterness and resentment.

Tumours develop their own blood supply, stealing life from the body. Similarly, sin finds ways to feed itself, throwing off constraints and finding new ways to feed its growing desires.

We are all diseased with the cancer of sin. The sooner we accept the fact that we need healing and bring our struggles into the open, the sooner we can heal. The great physician is waiting for us in his office. Not to scold us for being sick, but to heal us. To walk with us through the pain of removing our cancer and to limit its impact to this life, transferring his own health to us, and to give us ultimate and complete healing.

———◆———

Lord, we are sick, and we don't like to admit it. We cannot cure ourselves. We need you to heal us—to have you transfer your health to us and clean our bodies of the cancer of sin. Lord, do what you need to do in our lives to make us pure and healthy. We thank you that sin has no ultimate power over us, because you defeated it at the cross. So it is in your name that we pray. Amen.

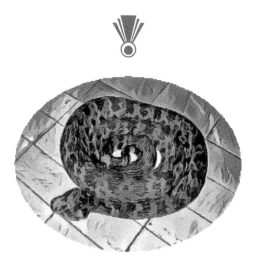

Cutting Open Sleepy Vipers

Five feet of rare Chinese viper stared, unblinking, through the glass of her enclosure. This lethal jade beauty had been a recent addition to the taxonomy of reptiles. Most large animals have been discovered and catalogued, but this stunning predator, with its emerald camouflage, had escaped detection by modern science by hiding in the underbrush of the remote mountains of central China.

"We are told it is one of the only vipers that can spit its venom!" the young reptile keeper said, beaming as I stared, my nose inches from the viper's face. "And because it is so rare, there is no antivenin."

I took a step back.

"And," he added with great pride, "it's worth a million dollars!"

A pale, little, worm-like appendage twitched at the tail end of her thick, shimmering body. It looked cute and innocent, as she wiggled it coyly hoping to attract unsuspecting birds and rodents. Staring at the appendage was an ominous triangular head with its cold unblinking eyes and hidden fangs. She was terrifyingly beautiful.

"See how one of her cheeks is larger than the other?" Dr. Yang asked.

I looked closely at her unbalanced cheeks. The swelling was most likely an abscess, but the only way to know for sure, or to treat it, was to lance it and allow the pus to drain out. But none of us were brave—or foolish—enough to work on her fully awake.

"I remember you told me that you use ether to anaesthetize reptiles. How exactly do you do that?" I asked.

"Well," he started thoughtfully, "we soak a big cotton ball with ether, put it in a clear plastic bin with the snake, close the lid and wait. Then, when it has fallen asleep, we open the lid and do our work—quickly—before it wakes up."

"I see. And how exactly do you know when it has fallen asleep?"

Dr. Yang rubbed his chin, "We kind of guess..."

That would be a problem.

"We do have this one thing!" he exclaimed suddenly, bounding out of the reptile hall and heading to the hospital pharmacy. "Maybe it will help. It was a gift to us from a foreign zoo, but we aren't sure how to use it," he added as he hurried along the hall.

He reached behind a jumble of old boxes in a corner beside the rickety wooden desk and pulled out a small cardboard box. Setting it on the table, he blew the dust off the cover, opened the lid reverently, and pulled out a shiny new isoflurane vaporizer. I grinned with delight! Isoflurane was the workhorse anesthetic of modern veterinary medicine. It produces few side effects, is well tolerated by almost any species, including birds and snakes, and has a wide safety margin. And this vaporizer represented the core, the critical beating heart, of an anaesthetic machine. I turned to Dr. Yang.

"This is fantastic. With this we can build our own anaesthetic machine," I said.

I carried the precious treasure back to my desk, set it down beside my laptop, and searched the internet for anaesthetic machine schematics, making a list of all the parts we were missing. We would need an oxygen tank, pressure regulator, flowmeter, some tubing, and

73

a few random clamps. We already had the oxygen tank, and with Director Li's permission, I spent the rest of the afternoon combing through local hardware stores for the hoses and clamps while she made phone calls on my behalf for other parts.

The following morning, Director Tong and I drove to the local human hospital and, with much pomp and ceremony, received an ancient anaesthetic system, which, at our request, they kindly donated to the zoo. It also saved the hospital the trouble of throwing it out.

Back at the zoo, I dug through the tool chest I had brought from home, and with some creative plumbing, we married the antiquated frame to the new vaporizer and stood back, lovingly admiring our Frankenstein creation. I could already imagine relaxed, stress-free surgeries, chatting calmly as we worked on comfortably snoozing patients. It would require some testing and calibrating, but in a few days, we would be ready to put it to use.

"In a few days" came rather suddenly when Director Tong, who rarely came to the veterinary hospital, appeared at my door later that afternoon.

"Dr. Paul, I have wonderful news," he beamed.

"Tomorrow we will do surgery on our viper snake. Isn't that exciting!?"

I stared at him.

"Now that we have the wonderful new anaesthetic machine you have what you need, right?" he said, raising his eyebrows. It was more of a statement than a question. "We have even arranged a TV crew to record it all."

A queasy fear stirred in my gut, and the room seemed to sway.

I feared for our precious patient. The machine had never been tested. We had no way of knowing if the percentage of anaesthetic on the vaporizer dial was accurate. And even if it was and there were no leaks and the machine lived up to our hopes, there was the issue of our lack of experience. How long would it take for the snake to fall asleep?

How would we know if it was asleep? How long would it stay that way? And even if we could do the procedure, we had no culture medium to grow the anaerobic bacteria that were likely causing the abscess. And then there was the issue of personal safety. My heart went out to the reptile keepers and my colleagues as I wondered which poor sod would be in charge of testing our new machine by working on this deadly viper. Director Tong interrupted my thoughts, puffed out his chest, and said, "And you, Dr. Paul, will be in charge of the anaesthesia, the examination, and the treating of the swelling."

Apparently, catching garter snakes as a boy and my general interest in reptiles was all the training necessary to do surgery on the mouth of a deadly pit viper.

I returned home, my mind filled with disturbing images but determined not to tell Michelle. There was no need to worry her. If I died, she would find out soon enough.

I did not sleep well that night.

The next morning, adrenaline coursed through my veins. All my senses were on high alert. I heard every footfall from the van to the office, saw every bird flitting in the trees, and noticed the pungent smell of antiseptic as I turned the rough knob of the hospital door.

We started by meeting with the team to go over the morning's plans. Dr. Yang, Director Li, and the young reptile keeper were already assembled.

"I want to let you know I am very concerned about the procedure this morning," I said, wondering how far I could push the issue culturally but keenly aware of the risks to my mortality. I started by pointing out the potential loss-of-face if things went badly. Public embarrassment for the zoo was a powerful card to play.

"The machine has not been tested. Our snake is precious, and we are not experienced with how reptiles will react to the anaesthetic yet. We also don't have the right culture medium to grow the most likely bacteria."

"I'm also concerned about our safety," I added, determined to move from general, public, "face-saving" to a more personal note.

Dr. Yang nodded gravely. Director Li gave a grunt of understanding, and the young reptile keeper's head bobbed silently. I searched each face, anxious for a response when I noticed a TV camera crew peaking in the door of the meeting room. Director Li looked up and brightened noticeably.

"Right, the media team is here. Time to get started," she said, smiling.

I had no choice but to move ahead but was determined that the preparation for the morning's procedure would happen slowly and methodically. After all, it was *my* life on the line.

"Dr. Yang, I need you to gather forceps, hemostats, scalpel blades, gauze, and iodine," I said, hoping to hit a commanding tone. "And can you carefully roll our anaesthetic machine to the reptile exhibit?" I asked the young keeper. "I'll follow shortly."

I quietly gathered the microscope slides, thinking about Michelle, who was at home, blissfully unaware of the whole thing, and said a prayer for us both.

In the chilly, grey, back room of the reptile exhibit, we set up a suitable treatment area for our endeavor.

"These hemostats have blood on them, and those forceps have bits of hair stuck to their handles," I pointed out to Dr. Yang. "We will need to get these cleaned up and sterilized with alcohol before we can proceed. And also, please bring a clean towel for us to lay them on."

Dr. Yang nodded and scurried off while I set up the microscope slides, syringes, and gauze. The reptile keeper appeared, jauntily wandering down the corridor with a large, clear, plastic container into which he had moved our hefty patient. He held the lid on tight, but even so, I thought him a very brave fellow. Dr. Yang returned, smiled, and carefully laid the now gleaming instruments on the clean towel beside us.

The camera crew was setting up for good angles, attaching cables to equipment, and holding light meters between myself and the box that held the viper. I tried to ignore them and leaned in to get a closer look at the lump we had to address, but when I noticed a video lens breathing down the neck of my lab coat, it became clear that the desire of the TV crew to get a good video was going to interfere with my desire not to die.

"Director Li, could I talk to you?" I asked, and motioned for her to step outside where we could speak in private. "Director Li," I said in the firmest voice I could muster, "Can you *please* have the camera crew step outside while we do the procedure?"

She smiled like a busy mom with a dull child and glanced past me at the open door, eager to get on with things.

I leaned sideways into her field of view and continued.

"If things don't go well, they will have footage of us killing this precious animal."

She looked at me, still smiling, and rubbed her chin.

"And I don't think footage of the foreign expert getting bitten and being rushed to the hospital writhing on a gurney would be very complimentary either."

She stopped smiling.

"Maybe you are right. Let's have them get shots before and after, and you can give an interview when it's all done."

The disappointed camera crew took a few "before" shots and shuffled out. Carefully, we attached the anaesthetic machine tube to the small hole in the plastic container, opened the oxygen valve to pressurize the system, and turned on the vaporizer. Nothing happened. A faint hissing sound let us know that gas was moving through the system, but the rest was a bit of a mystery. There was no time to worry about that. We had to trust that it was working and locked our eyes on our patient.

Snakes do not breathe quickly and can hold their breath for long periods. Our viper moved about her box suspiciously, licking the air with her tongue before she stopped and curled into a defiant lump, holding her breath.

Ten minutes passed.

"Do you think she is asleep?" Dr. Yang asked. "Or dead?"

"Not sure," I said.

"Let's poke her and see what happens."

We prodded her gently through a hole in the side using a long bamboo stick. Her side flinched ever so slightly. That was all, but it was enough. She was still awake.

Dr. Yang paced anxiously. I looked out the window, trying to make the time pass more quickly.

After forty agonizing minutes of waiting, prodding, and more waiting, we were confident enough to open the lid.

Cautiously, the keeper reached in and grabbed just behind her head, lifting it up as Dr. Yang hefted her limp, heavy body. Gently, I opened her mouth with blunt forceps and slid a thin plastic breathing tube into the airway that lay exposed on the floor of her mouth, careful not to brush the fangs that lay folded back against her upper jaw. With the tube in place and attached to the anaesthetic machine we closed her mouth and tied it gently with gauze.

Then came the moment we had all been waiting for. Gently, I pushed a needle into the lump and drew back on the plunger. Thick chunky pus filled the syringe. I smiled and looked at Dr. Yang.

"Just as we had expected," I said matter-of-factly, stifling an enormous sigh of relief. We lanced the abscess with a scalpel, flushed it with water and iodine and injected her with antibiotics.

The thick muscled body tightened. Time was growing short. One last flush of the wound, and it was time to put her back. We lifted the beautiful animal back into its cheap plastic box, removed the breathing tube, and closed the lid.

Carefully, I placed a sample from the syringe of pus onto a microscope slide. Then I took my microscope slides and walked out into the main exhibit hall to meet with the anxiously waiting camera crew. I explained what we had just done and had them follow me to the lab. I couldn't be upset with them. They had been doing their jobs, so for their sake, we made a special effort to line up good shots. We stained the slides liberally with the pretty blue and red dye and then leaned intently over the microscope, doing our best to look very scientific. By noon, the camera crew was satisfied with the footage they had captured and left.

For the rest of the day the world seemed to be a happy place. There was an air of lightness in the lunch room that afternoon. The birds outside the window sang just a little louder, the sun was a little happier, and the subtle flavours of my leftover spaghetti lunch came through with special vibrancy as I looked out the window, basking in the relief and joy... of escaping death.

But I am afraid that just as Eve was deceived by the serpent's cunning,
your minds may somehow be led astray from your sincere and pure
devotion to Christ. 2 Cor. 11:3
For Satan himself masquerades as an angel of light. 2 Cor. 11:14b

———◦———

Satan is a deadly presence in this world. But there is a common misconception that he tromps about, presenting himself as a terrifying specter, and that if we saw him, we would recognize the danger and flee. But he is far more cunning. Like a viper, he will appear iridescent, captivating, and beautiful—catching and holding our gaze, and then luring us in. His intent however, is our destruction and at the other end of his innocent-looking enticements are fangs of deadly poison. If you are being lured toward something that you know is wrong, regardless of how tempting, innocent or desirable it looks, run the other way before you come within striking distance of his fangs.

———◦———

Lord, open our eyes. Make us aware of the enemies' schemes. Don't let us be lured into things or situations that would draw us away from you. Lord, we are weak-willed and we ask that you do not lead us into temptation. But if we do find ourselves tempted, give us the strength to stand up under it and resist the devil. Help us to submit ourselves to you and resist the devil so that he will flee from us. Lord we look to you. Amen.

Blow Darts and Babies

I t was Friday again, and the week had raced by. After a brief morning meeting, we set off to various parts of the zoo. Dr. Lin would inject a small, flighty tufted deer with a blow dart to treat an infection. Dr. Yu went to check on our viper and inject her with antibiotics using a long pole syringe, and the others sauntered to their respective patients.

I followed Dr. Yu to see the viper. She was doing much better. The jaw swelling was smaller, but it was no longer draining. I feared it would re-fill and need to be lanced again. The snake raised its head and glared defiantly, daring us to have another go. Having a staring contest with a viper was unnerving—they don't blink. I decided to visit the turtles. They were much more neighborly.

I left the reptile exhibit and made my way to the deer where my good friend Dr. Lin was quietly creeping up on his quarry. He crouched behind a bush, raised the blow tube to his lips, and sent a little deer scampering with a syringe dart in its hindquarters, which fell out after a few bounces. Dr. Lin stood up to retrieve it. Darting animals, I learned, was delicate work. It's not only aim that matters, but how hard you blow. Thick-skinned animals require a good hard strike, while fragile baby deer, though fast and skittish, require a delicate touch. This was an aspect of veterinary medicine that was completely new to me. My farm and pet patients, even those who were not very happy to see me, were approachable, and I could, at the very least, touch them to examine them. At the zoo, however, very few animals could be touched without sedation. They were surrounded by people but were still wild animals. Some were too flighty to approach, and the rest were quite happy to bite, poison, kick, scratch, or, in the case of the elephants, step on you.

After lunch, Dr. Lin sat in his office and held his cheek and groaned. He complained of a toothache.

"Go home," I said. "I'll help with darting the deer this afternoon."

He nodded appreciatively and walked down the hall to ask Director Li. As soon as he left, I realized that I had never darted an animal with a blow tube and that the baby deer was a particularly small quarry to start with. I needed practice.

I filled a syringe with water to give it weight, put a needle tip on one end, a feathery red string tail on the other, and stepped outside. A small roll of old carpet rested bound and moldy against a back wall. *Perfect!* I thought as I set it up. I stepped back ten paces and held the blow tube up to my mouth. Steady... aim... BLOW. The dart flew limply through the air and bounced off the concrete, halfway to the carpet. *Hmmm....* I thought. *This is not easy!*

I tried again. The tree just left of the target got a dose of water injected into its bark. The bushes behind cringed as I set up to try again. Blow, miss, retrieve... Blow, miss, retrieve. After some time, this disheartening pattern was broken by an occasional hit. I was making progress.

Tong Ya, our local veterinary assistant-in-training, came out to watch. He was a helper and learning about the trade and, for the most part, only watched procedures. I offered him the blow tube. He smiled and waved me off.

"I have never done that."

"Have a go!" I insisted, quite happy to give my diaphragm a rest.

He picked up the tube, set up, and pierced the carpet dead center.

"Beginner's luck," he said with a shy smile.

I set a dry leaf on the carpet and gave him back the blow tube. He set up again and blew. Shattered leaf confetti floated to the ground, silently mocking me.

We started to take turns, and an obvious pattern emerged. His darts flew straight and true, while mine found rocks, twigs, and bushes in the yard. After some more practice, we went in for a drink of water. Both my lungs and my ego were getting tired.

That afternoon we went to the tufted deer enclosure. Even at full size, these deer were not much bigger than a medium-sized dog. Our patient was the size of a big cat. We loaded our dart and watched as it eyed us from behind a bush, nervously sniffing the air. Silently, Tong Ya handed me the blow tube. Even though I had more faith in his ability, the job was mine.

I stepped quietly into the pen, the clunky foreigner trying to be the unobtrusive bushman as I snuck around, crept over, set up, aimed, and blew. Bullseye! The dart hit his hind quarters exactly where I had hoped. But sadly, in my effort not to miss, I forgot the fragile nature of my target. The little deer yelped and bounded off on three legs, whining pitifully. *Funny, they never did that for Dr. Lin,* I thought. Then he stopped beside a low bush and stared at the wall, wide-eyed and shivering, so distracted by the pain that he allowed me to walk up to him and pull the needle out of his thigh without moving. I felt terrible. My moment of elation deflated by the sick realization that my enthusiasm had caused so much pain. The deer scampered off, still on three legs, to find his mother.

I shuffled out of the enclosure, trying not to make eye contact with the keepers who were anxiously observing the goings-on. Most keepers develop a close relationship with their animals, many of whom they have cared for from birth. They are not impressed with vets who cause unnecessary pain to their babies. I stood beside them quietly as we watched. Tenderly, the little deer tested its hind leg, gently touching its tiny hooves to the dirt. The keeper beside me breathed deeply, satisfied that his little one would recover from my crude attempt at darting, and turned away to attend to his duties. I had gotten the job done, but it had come at a cost. Clearly, I would need to nurture the tender side of this new skill.

Therefore, as God's chosen people, holy and dearly loved, clothe yourselves with compassion, kindness, humility, gentleness, and patience. Col. 3:12

———◉———

Tenderness, kindness, and gentleness are often dismissed as an unnecessary waste of time in our efficient "git 'er done" world. Results and numbers are often the top priority, and that attitude can creep into the church. God, however, places a high value on softer, more intangible traits. The fruit of the Spirit are not efficiency, attendance numbers, and results. God lists them as "love, joy, peace, patience, kindness, goodness, faithfulness, gentleness and self-control," and none of those can be counted or measured. God wants everyone to have a relationship with him, so he wants us to share our faith. But the results of our witnessing, that is his domain. He can reach people, with or without us. But in his grace, he invites us into his work, labouring alongside him, and sharing our faith with our neighbours. But to do that well we need to be dressed for the job. So, he reminds us to "clothe yourselves with compassion, kindness, humility, gentleness and patience."

———◉———

Loving, heavenly Father. Teach us to be kind and tender like you—making time for the sick, inviting children into your presence, and caring for the hurting. Help us to make it our top priority to be like You. We want to live out your qualities of compassion, kindness, humility, gentleness, patience, faithfulness, peace, joy, and love so that those around us will see your light shining through us. Teach us to be strong in you, but also tender and kind. Lord, we want the world to see you, and how wonderful you are, so it is for your glory's sake that we pray. Amen

Mandrills, Curtains, Phone Calls, and Fatigue

The young mandrill is still sick," Dr. Lin said as we walked down the hallway to morning rounds.

I was still concentrating on my granola breakfast bar, a special treat I refused to be distracted from, but nodded to let him know I was listening as my mind drifted back to our sweet little patient.

She first caught our attention leaning wearily against the wall of her cage while the others in her troop scampered about, her sorrowful expression deepened by the heavy bags of swollen skin under her eyes. The skin over her legs, arms, and abdomen was thick and swollen and left a finger imprint when we pressed on it. *Pitting edema* they called it in vet school, caused by a lack of protein in the blood, which allowed fluid to collect under the skin. After that initial exam, the little monkey had been treated with albumin to keep more fluid in its proper place inside the blood vessels, and though the results after each treatment were encouraging, it was a band-aid measure. The ultimate root of the problem remained a mystery. Blood had been taken during the first exam and showed a low red blood cell count and low blood protein but not much else.

We had used gentle restraint to examine the elegant little creature when we first treated her, but now that we had a functioning anesthetic machine it was decided that we would do a more thorough physical exam. Tang Ya rolled our fancy apparatus into our treatment room and laid the instruments and syringes out neatly beside it on a shiny metal table. Then we waited for our patient, admiring the table, the gleaming instruments, and the new machine. It all felt very professional.

A keeper wandered in carrying a cardboard packaging box clearly labeled "space heater" with a diagram of a heating unit.

Oh good, I thought, admiring his foresight in providing a heater for the mandrill during anesthetic and quietly wishing I had thought of it myself.

He opened the box, reached in, and pulled out our mandrill. No one else seemed surprised.

We put our patient on the table and positioned the anesthetic mask. She struggled only a little, fluttered her eyes, and fell asleep.

Our first task was to find a vein. I felt her saggy skin, closing my eyes and palpating for thin threads of blood under the sponge of edema. After fifteen minutes of fruitless squinting, poking, and prodding, we had turned our little dear into a pincushion. I was glad she was asleep. For the next fifteen minutes, every vet in the department took turns searching for tiny thready veins winding their way under thick boggy skin.

Early in the procedure, as other vets had a go and I stretched my sore back, I had received a call on my cell phone. Mr. Bau, the driver who took our kids to school, phoned to let us know he would be a little late picking them up. An extra twenty minutes was his guess.

I called Michelle.

We talked it over and decided that making other arrangements would be too much of a hassle. Michelle called the school to let them know. She got a hold of the mother of one of Luke's friends, who graciously offered to wait at the gate with our little ones.

While I was still on the phone with Michelle, the long-awaited curtain-delivery guy arrived at our house. It was a most inopportune time to hang our huge living room curtains.

Time passed.

Half an hour after the scheduled school pickup time, I called Mr. Bau. He was stuck in traffic. About another fifteen minutes, he suggested. Michelle called the waiting mom and apologized. Then she called me. The curtains were a foot too long and much too wide on one window and several inches too short on the other. She asked what she should do.

The Mandrill was still sleeping, and we had no more luck getting blood.

Mr. Bau called again. "Only about another ten minutes now," he said.

That would make him a full hour late.

I called Michelle.

She called the waiting mom and apologized once more. The curtain guy suggested we wash the curtains and see if they would shrink.

"Won't that make the one that is already too short even shorter?" Michelle asked.

"Try it and see," he suggested.

Mr. Bau called. He was now at the school. I called Michelle to let her know. She called the other mom and thanked her profusely for waiting for an hour with our kids.

By now the Mandrill had been asleep for over an hour. I suggested we wake her up.

The curtain guy wanted to know if he could leave. Michelle was not very happy. Washing the huge heavy curtains would be almost impossible for us, and in the end, even if the one shrank to the right size, the other would be too short.

"Just try it," the curtain guy pleaded.

"Fine, we'll try," Michelle conceded grudgingly.

Relieved, the curtain guy rushed out the door.

The kids got home.

Mr. Bau apologized.

"Being late can happen," she told him. "But if we had known it would be an hour the kids could have gone to their friend's house to wait."

She was gracious but clear.

The Mandrill was now awake and back in her heater-box transport cage.

I went home.

At dinner, all the kids wanted to tell me the big news: Mr. Bau had been late!

Michelle and I talked about the curtains. We called the company to tell them that washing the huge curtains would not be easy for us.

"Oh, it is not easy for us either," they replied. "So just try it."

What would we do? As we talked, a strange burnt odor filled the room. Michelle jumped up and ran to the kitchen. I followed. The wonderful pork loin that was simmering for supper had boiled dry and was rapidly turning into a burnt offering. Luke crawled around on the floor.

"What are you doing?" we asked.

"I'm staying under the smoke," he said. "We learned this at the school fire drill."

We threw out the pork and opened all the windows in the house to clear the smoke. There went supper.

We decided to walk to our neighbour to ask what we should do about the curtains. We wanted to be culturally appropriate.

"Oh, absolutely send it back. If it is not right, that is their problem," he said.

We went back home to call the curtain store, determined to be polite but firm.

"Fine, we'll pick it up tomorrow," he agreed.

Making these phone calls was exhausting.

I went out to buy fried rice from our local street vendor. The blue haze in the house slowly faded as we ate dinner. Then it was time for homework, diapers, stories, prayers, and bed for the kids, along with supper dishes and clean up. By eight o'clock we fell into bed and stared at the ceiling. Life, with all its adventures, was turning out to be quite tiring, but by his grace we were making it through.

In their hearts humans plan their course, but the Lord establishes their
steps. Proverbs 16:9
Many plans are in a man's heart, but the purpose of the LORD will
prevail. Proverbs 19:21

———⬥———

None of us knows what our day will hold when we wake up in the morning. It could be exciting or boring, wonderful or devastating. We make our plans for the future—and God encourages us to do so [Proverbs 6]. But our steps, as Solomon reminds us, are in his hands. We make plans, but his purposes prevail. That can feel ominous, as if God toys with us like a giant chess master, but his purposes for us, as well as our steps, are established by his *love* for us. He loves us so much that he is willing to walk with us through every "change of plans." God may even allow our plans to fail, but he remains in control and loves us beyond our wildest fancies. What a relief when we realize that the glorious adventure of our lives is directed by the one who loves us most.

———⬥———

Lord, sometimes our lives take a sudden turn, and we are tempted to doubt your love for us... or we doubt your power to intervene on our behalf. Strengthen our faith when our carefully laid plans suddenly come crashing down. Call us to you, our refuge, and remind us that whatever you have allowed in our lives is for your glory and our ultimate good. Lord when that ultimate good is hard to see, help us to look to the cross, where you demonstrated the full extent of your incredible love. Let the earth and all its problems and struggles grow dim as we look upon your glory and grace. Thank you for loving us and walking through this life alongside us. We love you. Amen

Media Frenzy

It was the day of the big media campaign. The zoo had graciously been waiting for me to adjust before inviting the media to do interviews, but it had been long enough. The time had finally come to show off their shiny new foreign vet. I had been informed a day in advance that this would be the big day, so I dressed in the cleanest of my four long-sleeved shirts (the rest of our clothes were in the much-delayed crate en route to China) and headed to the zoo.

Walking to the main office, I pictured a couple of reporters and one man with a camera waiting for me. However, as I approached the meeting room, my ears caught the animated voices of a press mob. Four TV stations, complete with video teams and smartly dressed reporters, and journalists, representing several newspapers, were all crowded in a little room. Director Tong sat beaming on his overstuffed chair in the middle of the entourage. He seemed particularly pleased.

"This is our famous Dr. Paul," he announced to the crowd. He stood up, put one arm over my shoulder, and shook my hand. It was a moment meant to convey friendship and welcome. Director Tong was not new to media events.

Cameras clicked and whirred, and reporters with little notepads scribbled notes and fired questions.

"Where are you from?"

"Why did you come to Cheng-Du?"

"How much money do you make?"

"Do you like it here?"

"What do you think of spicy food?"

"Do you play Majong?"

It all felt a bit surreal.

Mercifully, after the initial barrage of questions, at the direction of Director Tong, we stepped from the cramped meeting room to go make our way to a photo-op. Two lemurs had gotten into a scrap and needed tending to. A gaggle of reporters followed behind, continuing to ask questions and scrawling in their notepads. Others ran ahead to set up for a shot as I rounded a corner or walked down a picturesque path under a bamboo grove.

At the lemur exhibit, the crowd slowed and we squeezed into the little workroom behind the main cage to see our patient.

Injecting a gentle little lemur with antibiotics was not a big job, and certainly not worthy of a media frenzy, but the number of cameras and newspaper personnel that crammed into the stuffy little room made it feel like the great helmsman himself was being treated. The room got warm, camera crews jostled for position, reporters continued with their barrage of questions, a keeper tried to mop up the unsightly poop that the terrified lemur had squeezed out—and I tried to look natural.

The seemingly innocuous little newspaper articles and TV segments that appeared a few days later caused other media organizations to take notice. Apparently foreign veterinarians and zoo animals made for an interesting and profitable combination. Sichuan TV, a nationally broadcast station that even showed in parts of Canada, wanted to do a ten-minute piece entitled "The Norman Bethune of the Chengdu Zoo."

Who was Norman Bethune? He was a national hero in China. A doctor (the human kind) who had come from Canada to aid the Chinese army during their war with Japan. He was also the subject of a famous poem by chairman Mao and was touted by the Communist party as a folk hero to be revered and emulated. Every man, woman and child in China had heard of him. In Canada, he was almost unknown.

Even though I was Canadian, I felt very uncomfortable being compared to the exalted Norman Bethune. It seemed odd to me that the media would take such an interest in a simple Canadian vet who had come to live in China with his family. But as a foreigner with four children, the intrigue of my work at the zoo, and the potential of a Panda thrown in for good measure, I could see how it could make for an engaging story.

Director Tong visited the veterinary hospital later that afternoon after the last of the media had drifted away.

"That was great! They loved you and you have brought great honour to our zoo," he said delightedly. "And it brings us lots of free advertisement," he added with a wink.

He was going to capitalize on this aspect of his new hire, and I couldn't blame him. The zoo needed the revenue and exposure, and I was a great way to do that. And anyway, our desire to play a discreet, low-key role in China had vaporized with this first media crew, so I had to accept that I was the poster child for the zoo and did my best to adjust to this new role.

Several days later the Sichuan TV crew arrived to spend the day with me. An energetic young man with bright eyes and slick hair jumped out of the van. His cameraman was right behind him, one eye pressed against the eyepiece of the video camera on his shoulder, filming the introduction.

"Nice to meet you, teacher," he said. "We are *so* excited to be here. I have never interviewed a foreigner before. Can I see a picture of your family? Do you like spicy food? We can't wait to see what you do! What is Canada like? I brought lunch!"

It was going to be a long day.

We started with me driving in through the main gate like I did every day when I arrived for work.

"Please back out and drive in again," the camera guy said as he set up to shoot from a different angle. We repeated it several times.

We repeated this charade throughout the day. Stand here, pose there, read a book, look deeply concerned, fill a syringe, talk to the Panda...

On our way back from the pregnant giraffe (her belly was still getting bigger), I noticed a caterpillar desperately hurrying to cross the walkway before getting trampled. I bent over and placed it on a juicy clump of grass.

"Don't you know that is a pest?" the reporter asked, "Why would you save it?"

"Well," I replied, "I am an animal doctor, and that is an animal. Also, he is not aware that we call him a pest, and no one will complain when he turns into a butterfly."

For the first time that day, the young man shuffled long in silence, trying to understand the curious foreigner who wanted to save a garden pest. In the end, he decided to film the sequence just in case he figured it out later.

"You go ahead and video us walking down the path," he instructed the cameraman. Then he combed the bushes looking for another caterpillar. His search came up empty, which, given the liberal way the gardeners sloshed around pesticides, was not a surprise. He chose a brown, dead, curled-up leaf as a stand-in (a fitting choice under the circumstances) and gently laid it on the path in front of me.

"Let's you and I walk along this path again and redo that sequence."

Then, as if to let me in on a secret he leaned in and whispered, "You can pick up the dead leaf. Just pretend it is a caterpillar. No one will notice."

We reshot the sequence until eventually, after many takes, the leaf disintegrated.

"It's almost five o'clock," the reporter noted, looking at the leaf dust and the cameraman, whose eyes were pleading to go home. "Time to wrap up."

On the drive home I pondered the balance between the allure of fame and the desire to blend into the crowd. One is driven by pride and the desire for personal recognition, the other by fear, or false humility, or laziness. And either one, taken to the extreme, is a problem.

What do you have that was not given to you? And if it was given to you,
why do you brag as if you did not receive it as a gift? 1 Cor. 4:7
Each of you should use whatever gifts you have received to serve others, as
faithful stewards of God's grace in its various forms. 1 Peter 4:10
So do not be like the Pharisees. Everything they do is for people to see.
Matthew 23:5

———— ◉ ————

Some of us desire fame. We want to be recognized and honoured. But that glory belongs to God alone. As the giver of our abilities, our appearance, and our talents, he alone deserves the credit for who we are and the things we accomplish.

On the other hand, some of us take the talents God has given us and hide them behind our backs because we don't want the work they may create, or the attention they might produce. We may be driven by laziness, fear of failure, or false humility. This too robs God of his glory because he can't display what he is doing through us.

So, let us enjoy using our gifts freely and without hesitation, but never with pride or a spirit of self-seeking, lest we touch his glory.

———— ◉ ————

Heavenly father, we humbly recognize that everything we have—our talents, our abilities, our resources, even this incredible body of ours—is a gift from you. Help us enjoy these gifts, care for them, and develop them, so that we might point to you through them and honour you as the great gift-giver. And Lord, if we are tempted to take credit for ourselves, stop us, lest we touch your glory. And when we hide your gifts out of a false humility, because we are afraid of failure, or because we are just plain lazy, stir us up to put them to use. For your glory's sake we pray. Amen.

Treasures from Home

It had been a long wait. Three months to be precise. Temperatures and autumn leaves were dropping when our shipment finally arrived. The four long-sleeved shirts and one sweater I had packed in the summer (when long-sleeved shirts were not part of my wardrobe) had seemed like too many at the time. *Surely our shipment will follow us in a few weeks, so I'll only need t-shirts and shorts,* I had thought.

But I was not the only one making do. Michelle had brought mainly breezy summer blouses, and we had not packed many sweaters for the kids. Coats, hats, and mitts were all in the crates, as were toys—and *that* was a problem.

Fortunately, Michelle had carefully planned our kids' backpacks for the initial thirteen-hour flight. An extra set of clothes, for "just in case," was squeezed on the bottom. Next was a little bag of cheerios and some granola bars for snacking, and finally some toys. "You may each pick a toy or two, a *small* stuffed animal, and a few small books," she had told our little ones. Rachel, our little artist, had also insisted on some colouring pencils and paper.

These few toys were pressed into service for the next three months. Little plastic dinosaurs served as space men, empty cardboard boxes filled many hours, and Rachel's baby doll did clandestine work as a superhero. Rocks and sticks from outside became army men, and simple imaginary games were elevated to new heights of complexity.

On the cooking front, Michelle did a remarkable job of serving up tasty meals using minimal spices, only one pot, one pan, and exactly six forks, knives, and spoons. She had packed these and a few plastic breakfast plates "just in case." I had mocked her at the time but was most grateful for them as the days dragged on.

At the zoo, I was flying blind. No books, no tools, and no exotic animal experience. Some foreign expert! I tried to look things up on the internet, which was frustrating at best, and had to email North American zoo vets to ask even the most basic of questions. It was embarrassing, and as the days got shorter my frustration grew.

But on this day—this grand day—everything was different! I sat in my office perusing the many boxes and packages and smiled. Dr. Lin sauntered in, settled into a chair, and started poking through the packages on the table.

"These are nice surgical tools," he said, picking up a shiny pair of hemostats.

"Yes, these are German, and those are from the USA," I replied, picking up another pair. "See how well they lock when you squeeze the handles?"

Dr. Lin squeezed, listening to the satisfying click of precision craftsmanship.

"And these are suture packs. They are pre-sterilized and have the needle already attached to the suture," I said, fanning out a full set in various sizes.

"And this," I said, holding up Fowler's *Zoo Animal Medicine*, "is the epitome of exotic animal veterinary books. It is the go-to reference for us zoo vets."

It was an older edition, but I presented it like the life-saving source of information that it was and opened the book.

"You see, it has chapters on primates and reptiles, seals and elephants," I pointed out. "And here are reference tables with detailed normal blood values for langur monkeys and different birds and such."

Dr. Lin smiled and nodded appreciatively.

"And when we have questions, you can read it and tell us what it says," he said, leafing through the pages with all their complex English words.

Back at home, life had taken on a festive atmosphere. Kitchen cupboards held mugs and real plates, and the drawers were filled with serving spoons, knives, and ladles. The bookcases sprang to life with colourful children's books, and dresser drawers received warm socks, more underwear, and much-anticipated cozy sweaters.

The kids arrived home from school and were immediately absorbed by the rediscovery of favourite toys. Luke built a Lego castle, complete with a drawbridge and a moat. Isaac set up his stuffed animals in order of size and colour just so that he could admire them. Rachel had a tea party for her dolls, telling them animated stories about her morning at kindergarten, and James had rescue heroes attempting courageous feats of derring-do from his dresser to his bed. On Saturday morning, by the time Michelle and I got up for breakfast, the kids had already played Candyland, Mouse Trap and Monopoly.

As we sipped our morning coffee, cupping our newly arrived mugs in both hands, feeling their warmth and delighting in the smooth ceramic on our lips, I wondered if I had ever really been grateful for them. Mugs had just been things I reached for and used unthinkingly. So were sweaters and warm socks. Now these were all treasures to be cherished and appreciated. I placed the mug on the table, careful not to chip an edge, and admired it lovingly.

How often, I thought, *have I done the same with my wife or my kids? Taking them for granted, not recognizing the treasure that they are?* I glanced at the Bible on the bookshelf. *And how often have I done that with you or (gulp) your author?*

I seek you with all my heart; do not let me stray from your commands. I have hidden your word in my heart, that I might not sin against you.

Psalm 119:11

—————◉—————

The Bible is one of those treasures that we seem to take for granted. Many of us have multiple copies, in various translations, so having God's word at hand seems normal and expected. Reading it can get routine and dare we say, even dull. Like a familiar coffee mug, it is just kind of there, underappreciated and left on the shelf as we wander by.

In Psalm 119, that famously long chapter of the Bible, the psalmist reflects on the value of God's word. He rejoices in it "as one rejoices in great riches." He meditates on it, delights in it, promises not to neglect it, loves it, and points out its many benefits. Maybe by making this Psalm about the word of God the longest chapter in the Bible God is trying to tell us something. Maybe it's time to reengage with God's word, treasure it, and have it daily be that lamp to our feet, a light for our path, and the warm glow in our souls.

—————◉—————

Heavenly Father, like so many of the gifts you provide, we can so easily take the gift of your word for granted. Help us to remember what a treasure it is. That there are many in the world who don't own a Bible, even though they wished they had one. Lord, your word is of greater value than any riches. It is the ultimate teacher and guide for life and is the clearest revelation of yourself that you have given us. Help us to use it to discover who you are in new and deeper ways. Use it to draw us to you. As the psalmist says, "Open my eyes that I may see wonderful things in your law," so that our lives might better reflect your glory. Amen

Ready, Aim... Vaccinate

Hoof and mouth disease carries with it a sense of doom. It's a withering illness, highly infectious, and able to devastate entire herds. Intensive vaccination programs had eradicated it in many countries, but it was still prevalent in many parts of China.

It was a crisp autumn day. Golden gingko leaves drifted onto the walkways as our little entourage made our way through the zoo to vaccinate every deer, antelope, and elk—anything with split hooves. It was a job that required a coordinated effort by a crew of staff and keepers, as well as a healthy supply of injection darts.

My first experience with darts had not been a great triumph, but I was determined to improve. At the hospital, Director Li, in her usual stiletto heels; my grinning friend, Dr. Lin; the quiet Dr. Yu; Dr. Wu, the cool carnivore guy; and Tang Ya, our intern, had prepared for the expedition. Bottles of vaccine, cotton swabs, darts, and needles were piled into our little plastic picnic baskets. Next, we chose our weapons. I had reached for the fancy imported weapon with a shy grin, and they, kindly, pretended not to notice as they picked up their plastic blow-tubes. Then we set off to the enclosures where elk, addax, David's deer, muntjac and other hoof-stock milled about.

My companions sent the first round of darts flying over the cobbles of the elk enclosure and turned to me, smiling mischievously. Word had gotten around about my darting skill. I loaded a dart, dialed up the pressure on the dart gun, aimed at the ample backside of a big bull, squinted my eyes, and squeezed the trigger. The bull scampered across the yard, the dart bouncing merrily in his rear until it fell out and landed, empty and unharmed on the cobbles. Everyone smiled.

This will be fun, I thought as we loaded up again when, invigorated by my success, I decided to propose a wager.

"How about if the one who misses the most this morning treats everyone else for lunch?"

"Sure! Yes! Great idea! Excellent suggestion," they said.

Their enthusiasm was unsettling.

My experience with darts had left a lot to be desired, and I was questioning my knee-jerk wager, especially after they all agreed so readily, but once it was said, I couldn't really take it back.

We started taking turns.

Each hit was followed by a joyous cry of relief. "Woohoo, I'm not treating for lunch!"

After three rounds, the score was tied. No one had missed, and the tension was beginning to mount. It was my turn again.

The darts we used were homemade and not crafted to quite the same specifications as the original imported ones. They worked—sort of—and were a fraction of the price, but required a bit more finesse. I had not taken into account the thinning tail of the dart I was using and did not dial enough pressure on the gun when I set up, aiming for the thigh of a bull elk, a particularly large target.

"Floooofffff" went the gun as the air from the canister puffed around the dart in the barrel, which sailed limply through the air and skidded to a halt at the feet of the big bull. He looked at the dart and then at the pathetic foreigner before he wandered off, thoughtlessly crunching the syringe under his hooves.

A joyful cry went up from the others. "Paul's treating for lunch. Paul's treating for lunch!"

"Hold on a minute," I said. "We still have lots of animals to dart, so this isn't over!"

Everyone smiled supportively, but they seemed far too happy as they filled more syringes and, one by one, all hit their targets. Then all eyes turned to me.

Determined not to have the same limp display, I dialed the pressure up, stuffed a cotton ball in the barrel for good measure, and determined to aim a little high to account for gravity. A yearling elk stood in front of a concrete wall at the back of the pen. I crept up, took careful aim, and fired.

BANG!

The dart missiled out of the barrel and exploded on the wall behind my target like a firecracker. The elk jumped, and a happy cry went up.

"Paul is treating for lunch. Paul is treating for lunch!"

Things were not looking good for me. After a few more second-rate attempts I decided not to waste any more vaccine and made myself useful by loading darts instead of injecting walls and cobblestones.

Six of us strolled to lunch at the little restaurant just outside the gates of the zoo that day. My colleagues were polite, but between mouthfuls of fried pork ribs and spicy tofu, they commented quite happily on how much tastier things were when someone else was buying. But the few dollars spent on lunch were well worth the camaraderie and deepening friendship, not to mention the lesson in humility. We returned to the hospital a happy, satisfied crew.

Only half the hoof stock had been vaccinated that morning and most of my coworkers attended a Communist party training session in the afternoon, so on the following morning Dr. Lin, Tang Ya, and I set off to vaccinate the remaining deer.

I was determined not to give up on my dart gun and started the new day with a revived sense of confidence. I had learned a lot the day before. With one dart in the barrel of my gun and three more in my pocket, I stepped into the fallow deer enclosure. Set up, aim, shoot. The first dart was a solid hit. I smiled.

Four darts later, I still had not missed and was starting to get a feel for the whole dart business. We continued to load and shoot. After fifteen shots and fifteen hits, I was enjoying a vigorous sense of confidence.

Dr. Wu had finished his rounds and came sauntering by.

"Want to bet again?" he asked hopefully.

"Sure!" I shot back with a confident grin.

My confidence roused suspicion.

"You seem very sure of yourself."

"Fifteen shots, Fifteen hits!"

"Oh," he paused, "never mind then."

The last animals left to vaccinate were the takin. These rare Himalayan creatures were particularly majestic. Their short, curved horns gave them the Chinese name *Niu Jiao Ling* or "turned-horn deer." They are part of the goat family, but are large, weighing several hundred pounds. Their front legs are longer than their back legs, which gives them the unusual stance of a hyena. A heavy-set black snout, wheat-coloured coat, and shaggy mane finishes off the look. I watched and marveled. An ominous deep gurgle rumbled, like distant thunder, from the chest of the big male. I set up and fired. He responded to the dart by charging defiantly at the fence. Pride glinted in his eyes and mist puffed from his flared nostrils as he pawed the ground in the crisp autumn air. *What an amazing creature*, I thought, hoping that our vaccination efforts, and the efforts of zoos around the world, would be able to preserve it and the many other animals at the zoo that so magnificently display God's creative genius.

God blessed them and said to them, "Be fruitful and increase in number;
fill the earth and subdue it." Genesis 1:28
The LORD God took the man and put him in the Garden of Eden to
work it and take care of it Genesis 2:15

———— ◉ ————

Genesis 1:28, where God commands his newly created humans to "subdue" the earth, is one of the more misunderstood passages in the Bible. God isn't commissioning mankind to be tyrannical pillagers of his creation. Rather, the idea of subduing the earth involves actively ruling over it to cultivate it, making the land productive, and life-sustaining. So, in Genesis 2, he clarifies our role regarding his new home as being to "work it and take care of it."

One of the ways that we honour God is by caring for and protecting this magnificent world that he created. He gives us the freedom to use it, frolic about in it, discover its many secrets, and enjoy it as his gift. But he also expects us to respect it and manage it well.

———— ◉ ————

Lord, thank you for allowing us to enjoy this incredible world that you have created. Its variety and creativity give us a small glimpse of your glory. We can't wait to experience more and more of it for all eternity. Forgive us for taking this world for granted, for treating it as if it is ours to exploit and abuse. Help us to respect it like the priceless piece of art that your creation is. Your invisible qualities—your eternal power and divine nature—are clearly seen and can be understood from what you have made. Show us how to protect your handiwork so that we might honour you, the great artist that created it all, and so that future generations might also be able to marvel at your work. For your glory's sake we pray. Amen.

More Monkey Trouble

Look, he's scratching his butt," the pudgy little jokester said, pointing at the monkey on the rock. The rest of Rachel's kindergarten class pressed their noses against the glass and giggled with impish delight. For now, this was the highlight of their day, but I was not to be upstaged by a bum-scratching monkey and a class clown. I had planned great and exciting things. I would take them to the lions next. That would be sure to impress!

I smiled at Michelle, who had joined the little entourage with James, toddling along beside her as we wandered on from the squirrel monkeys. There was much to see—a yawning lion, two feisty blue sheep butting heads over rights to the last crumbs of oats, and a peacock displaying his full regalia of finery, much to the delight of the children. It was turning out to be a splendid day at the zoo.

After the hippos, at the stone picnic tables in the shade of the bamboo grove, the class unpacked their lunches (peanut butter sandwiches or Korean kimbop, depending on who your parents were).

The kindergarten teacher leaned back toward my table.

"It's been a fun day. Thank you for the tour, but I think we need to head back to school."

"My stomach doesn't feel so good," Rachel mumbled quietly, looking up at her mother. "Can I stay with you guys?"

We looked at each other, and at the longing eyes of our little five-year-old. She loved the zoo, she loved being with mom and dad, and after the morning's excitement, what remained of the afternoon would be an academic wash anyway. We nodded to her, walked the class to the gate, waved our goodbyes to the grinning faces in the bus windows, and headed back to the office.

Rachel sank into a big black office chair and disappeared behind an anatomy book. James amused himself with rubber bands and a few old surgical clamps, while Michelle and I unpacked a few more boxes.

"Maybe we can head home a little early," Michelle suggested hopefully, as she arranged gauze packs on the shelf.

"I'd like that," I said. "It's been a long week and I could really use—"

Dr. Lin poked his head in the door.

"One of the monkeys on the hill has been injured. Can you come?"

I sighed. Michelle handed me a gauze pack and gathered the kids' belongings to head home while I grabbed iodine and suture needles and set them in my kit beside the gauze squares.

At the monkey house, we were presented with our patient, his sedated head draped miserably over the end of a wooden pallet and rested on the cement floor. I bent over the feeble little macaque steaming with polite rage. He was one of twenty-odd macaques that live on "monkey hill," a large natural-looking enclosure in the centre of the zoo. Macaques are highly social animals with a defined troop hierarchy. At times, one tries to usurp another on the social ladder, which usually results in a loud, vicious public brawl. My patient had been part of such a slugfest and came out rather poorly. But the skirmish was not what made me angry. It was the thick yellow puss and green rotting flesh flapping on the side of his skull where his scalp had been that infuriated me. This was an old injury. Much of his head was laid bare. There was a long gash on his back and two of his four thigh muscles had been torn in half, creating a deep chasm in his leg. How this injury could have gone unnoticed for so long was beyond me.

"Look!" I pointed out to the others, "The muscle is green. It stinks and pus is running down his fur. This is an old injury!"

I fought the urge to yell.

"Now we need to resect even more of his scalp in order to clean it up and we cannot suture any of his injuries. They are too badly infected."

I strapped on my headlamp to keep me from saying anything I might regret and got down to work.

Open wounds are tricky things. Six hours is about the limit to clean, suture, and close an injury. Beyond that, the bacteria in the wound have multiplied to a point where suturing only locks them in. This hides the injury and for a brief period all looks rosy. But the infection remains, grows, and forms an abscess, which if it does not kill the patient, erupts creating an even bigger problem. The only option is to start with debridement—a fancy medical term for merciless scouring of the wound.

I looked at my sad little patient, wondering where to start. A loose flap of hide hung from its head. Puncture wounds pierced the skin, oozing a slow syrup of pus. The muscle that remained looked like ripe avocado. It stunk. The scissors, scalpel blades, and other surgical equipment that had recently arrived from Canada would now be put to good use.

I leaned over his head and, like a sadistic barber, sliced away flaps of scalp. It felt unnatural and contrary to every instinct. Exposing flesh just seems wrong and exposing bone even more so. But dead tissue cannot be revived and only serves as fodder for more bacteria to grow. I snipped away, exposing more and more of my patient's head. Next, I took out the scalpel blade and rasped away at the skull, removing dried blood and dirt to reveal the clean white bone underneath. Next came the infected muscle remaining on the shores of the glistening white scalp. I clipped, cut, and scraped until only pink bleeding edges remained. There was now much more exposed skull, but the edges were clean and the infection had been removed.

In the meantime, Dr. Lin tended to the wound on his back and leg. Hesitantly he snipped away small bits of green or plucked away a few loose hairs with their forceps.

"Keep going. Be ruthless! Cut away all that dead stuff," I said, waving my hand at the wound.

Timidly, Dr. Lin trimmed a small sliver, looked up and raised his eyebrows looking for approval.

"Let me show you," I said, holding out my hand for the instruments.

Relieved, he placed the forceps and scissors in my hand and straightened his back. Holding the exposed end of the quadriceps muscle I cut away a solid chunk. Blood oozed from the fresh end.

"Bleeding edges like this are good!" I explained to the shocked faces staring down at me. "We can't leave any infection. Even if we remove a little healthy stuff, it's better than leaving any infection. It may look harsh, but it is the only way to save him."

I continued to slash away dead muscle and ladled copious amounts of water through the wound to remove any hidden pus and debris. Satisfied that the wound was clean, I pointed my light deep into the defect. At the bottom of the chasm, hope flowed through the ominously pulsing femoral artery. The whole thing would now be left open to close through second-intention healing. Bit by bit, the body would contract the wound, populating the edges with healthy cells and migrating them toward the centre. It would leave a significant scar, but it would heal.

As I rose and stretched my back, Dr. Lin placed him in a small cage and injected the anaesthetic reversal agent. Almost instantly the monkey stirred and sat up. He looked sad, but a little more put together, and there was a slight twinkle in his eyes. He peered up at us, reached for the basket of fruit outside of his cage, and grabbed a banana. Munching gently, one ear still hanging limply on the side of its head, he was ready to start the long battle toward recovery. The first skirmish was over, but the war would be a long one.

I arrived at work the next day, eager to get to monkey hill. I had grown attached to the little scrapper and was anxious to see him pull through.

"Let's not sedate him again and just give him some antibiotics," Dr. Lin suggested. It was the easier and more conservative approach, but the stench of rotting flesh was still fresh in my nostrils.

"No, we need to recheck and re-clean the wounds," I said firmly.

Reluctantly Dr. Lin loaded the dart. Moments later we pulled our sleepy client out of his cage to inspect the injuries. The head wound looked dry, and the edges sealed over, but a thin layer of pus had pooled in the pocket of skin at the base of its neck. We re-cleaned and flushed the wounds. Tentatively I placed a few sutures under the skin around his right ear, hoping to create enough adhesion to save it. The leg wound looked clean, but it was deep—very deep. Hair, food, and feces could all get stuffed into such a cavern. Covering the wound with bandages was not an option. Curious little minds and dexterous monkey fingers make quick work of even the most securely placed bandages. The only option was to try to reattach the two sides of the quadriceps muscle and reduce the depth of the wound. Under the watchful eye of Dr. Lin, I placed a tension-reducing suture on each end of the muscle and slowly edged the two sides together. If it worked, it would be a miracle.

"Very good, very nice," Dr. Lin said, smiling. I realized much of this was new for him, so I slowed down, taking time to explain surgical tricks. Then, having pumped his backside full of antibiotics, we put our patient back and reversed the anesthetic. Once again he sat up, and once again he reached for a banana. He was a fighter.

As we walked to check the pregnant giraffe, we discussed our case.

"That head lamp of yours is really useful. Did you bring that with you from Canada?"

"Oh, this lamp? I'm glad you asked," I said delightedly.

I was convinced that excellent medicine is possible with minimal tools, provided that you know how to make the most of them. Light always seemed to be in short supply in China, but it was critical for doing a good physical exam, proper wound management, or anything else one did with open eyes. I figured I looked a little odd with a lamp strapped to my forehead, but I was determined to use it, and as a foreigner, looking odd was expected.

"I got this light from an outdoor store here in town. It uses regular batteries, and only costs 60 yuan (about nine dollars)."

"That's great," my friend replied. "I think we should get one for everyone in the hospital." Like a travelling salesman I continued to sell the advantages of good lighting and the head lamp as we walked. Though the monkey situation was a frustration to me, some good had come out of it. If I could demonstrate the advantage of good lighting and the value of thorough wound cleaning, the whole thing would not be in vain. Steps were being taken, and infection was being beaten back.

If your hand or eye causes you to sin, gouge it out or cut it off. It's better to enter heaven maimed than to have the whole of you thrown into hell.
Matthew 5:29,30

———◉———

Some of Jesus' teachings seem hard—cruel even. Gouging things out or cutting them off seems unnecessarily harsh. But Jesus the great physician knows that untreated sin, like an infection, spreads to the healthy parts of life. Covering it up may hide it for a time, until it erupts with even worse consequences. And left unchecked, it kills. Slashing away all vestiges of sin from our lives seems harsh and excessive, but Jesus knows it is necessary. But radical surgery is hard, so we timidly snip away a little here or there, removing only the most obvious parts of sin. What we need is someone who will do it for us. One who will be radical with the cleaning. If we allow the light of Christ to shine into the deep recesses of our lives and allow his skilled, loving hands to cut away all the death that lurks within, he will cure us. The battle can be long and scars may remain, but in the end, there will be life.

———◉———

Lord, we are born with sin, infected in our wombs through our parents. And we have added to it through our own choices and actions. We thank you that we have the guarantee of ultimate complete healing because of your sacrifice on the cross, and we look forward to being completely "sin-disease" free. But until that ultimate victory over sin, we live in this fallen world and are affected by all its depravity. Lord, don't let our sin lure us away from you. Remove it before it spreads. Make us aware of how deadly it is and give us the courage to hand you the scalpel. Help us to see that any cutting or amputating you do in our lives is for our good. Jesus, you who knew no sin, were willing to become sin, so that we might be healed. We thank you for being our great physician, our Saviour, and our Lord. Amen

When a Panda Dies

The fancy imported pick-up truck, with its intricate panda logo on the side, backed effortlessly into the space in our humble vet department parking lot. I leaned over my desk and squinted through the window into the morning sun, shifting for a better look. This was no ordinary visitor. In China, if you had money and bought an imported vehicle, you didn't buy a pick-up truck—you bought a Mercedes. Who would spend that much on a pickup? My curiosity grew even more when I noticed the fuzzy black and white bulge in the truck bed.

"Is that a panda?" I yelled to Dr. Yang, who, to my surprise, had left his desk and was quietly leaning over my shoulder to stare out my office window.

"I think so," he whispered calmly in my ear.

"No way! That is so cool," I squealed, bolting for the door.

I realized as I ran down the hall that squealing with delight was not the proper response to a dead national treasure, but I felt I could be forgiven. I was a foreigner and this, after all, was a panda!

At the time, there were less than two thousand pandas left in the world, so each individual was important, especially the wild ones. Not only were they endangered, but they were China's national symbol, a powerful ambassador of the Middle Kingdom, filled with warmth, cuddly softness, and matchless rarity. They were icons of China that the government was keen to preserve—so keeping pandas alive (or determining the cause of death) was a matter of utmost national importance. This animal had been brought to the zoo rather than the official panda reserve just north of us because, if it happened to have died of an infectious condition, they did not want to expose any of their breeding stock. It was also an opportunity for the zoo to garner free advertising, so the media had been alerted.

I leaned over the truck bed, carefully inspecting the dusty black and white shag. Cautiously I reached out, rubbing the coarse black fur, wondering if by chance the bear might twitch.

Several keepers in crisp, blue, camera-ready overalls arrived to transport the bear from the truck to our little, white-tiled necropsy room. The rest of the veterinary department had been alerted, and we rushed back to our offices and donned our cleanest white lab coats, the ones without patches or blood stains. Then we hurried to the necropsy room and waited like mourners, with folded hands and appropriately grave expressions as the pallbearers walked by, lifted her gingerly onto the table, and stood back in reverent silence. Behind them on the shelves, a spectator gallery of fetal specimens in glass jars watched with vacant foreboding. The musty odor of damp dead bear mingled with the sharp sting of formaldehyde. No one smiled. It all had the aura of a state funeral. Zoo staff, camera crews and reporters, as well as a few curious groundskeepers shuffled quietly into our little room, adding to the grave, stuffy atmosphere. The stage had been set, and a heavy silence blanketed the audience as eyes and lenses focused on us, waiting for the curtain to rise.

Our job was to find the cause of death. Vague guesses would not suffice. Director Li, who, along with myself, had been chosen as the formal representatives of the hospital, looked at me and nodded. She had seniority and position and was dressed for the cameras in her usual cocktail dress and elegant heels. I had on dusty sneakers and old trousers but had education and a foreign face. Neither one of us had any experience doing panda necropsies.

Carefully we studied the bear, gently rolling her over to examine every side.

Her slender lips were bordered by the salt and pepper of old age. She was slight and frail, with a few old scars, but there were no major injuries. I had hoped for something obvious: a hidden wound, a bullet hole, or some bruising to give us a clue.

"She's old," I said to the young intern who was taking notes.

I blinked hard, ignored the sweat under my lab coat, picked up a scalpel and looked at Director Li as we weighed the gravity of our situation. Necropsies can be tricky detective work, and with our limited tools and lab equipment, there was a good chance we would not find an obvious cause of death. But in the Middle Kingdom, "I don't know" was not an acceptable answer from a well-paid foreign expert doing what he was supposedly trained to do. Cameramen leaned in as we prepared to make our first cut. Zoo director Tong, who had come to witness the event, smiled and stepped back to give the photographers a better angle, hoping that his investment in a Canadian vet would not disappoint him on national TV.

Parting the course white fur we made our first incision along the midline of the abdomen, gently pulling back the skin. There was no fat, just an emaciated layer of muscle on either side of the midline. Cameras, sweat, and nerves all faded away as we focused on our task. Carefully I pierced through the abdominal wall, ran my scissors along the white ligament running the length of the belly and spread the two sides. The internal organs were dry and tacky. At least we could say she was dehydrated. Not a headline-worthy discovery, but it was a start. Gently we widened the opening to explore the abdominal organs. The empty stomach was soft and normal. Maybe a bit more muscular than other animals, but then, it takes a lot to grind up bamboo. The liver seemed a normal colour and size, as did the smooth, flaccid bladder. No smell of infection. No evidence of widespread cancer. *Lord, let us find something,* I thought. The beads on my forehead were getting bigger, and I was afraid the cameras would catch me sweating into the national treasure. We needed to find something—anything would be fine—but we *were* hoping for spectacular. Dr. Li pointed to the large tangle of intestines. Gingerly we lifted and inspected each segment of small intestine, laying the pale loops reverently on the soft blanket of white fur. They looked completely normal. Inch by inch, the mound of intestines grew until—firmly attached to the duodenum—a thick, burgundy-black swelling rose to the surface. We had a diagnosis!

Director Li and I displayed the angry section of purple bowel, beautifully contrasted against our white-gloved hands, as the cameras clicked. It was hard to find a suitable expression. I settled on an awkward mix of relief at a clear diagnosis, and appropriate public sadness over the demise of a panda.

"*This*," she said slowly and gravely, "is an intussusception. One part of the duodenum has rolled inside the next section, resulting in a thick swelling that has blocked food from passing. See how dark and firm it is?"

She gently squeezed the bulge, her fingers easily tearing through the friable dead lining. Heads nodded, pens wrote furiously, and cameras whirred as they zoomed in to catch the drama. She poked a few more holes to make sure everyone got the shot.

"The abnormal section has swollen, cutting off the blood supply to this area. This—" she pronounced, pausing for effect—"is the cause of death!"

Intussusceptions cause tremendous pain and eventually rupture, literally tearing the bowels apart, resulting in an agonizing death. Fortunately, our frail old girl had been too weak for it to get to that point and had mercifully died before it tore.

We laid the angry swelling on the spaghetti blanket of pale bowel for contrast and stood back. Cameras clicked as they leaned in for a close-up. I stepped back, took a deep breath, and wiped the sweat from my forehead.

Slowly, the curious onlookers melted back into the zoo, reporters packed up their lenses, my colleagues shifted their focus to lunch, and I found myself alone with my thoughts and a dead panda. In the end, this rare priceless treasure was just another dead bear. If it had died in the wild, it would have been food for scavengers, fertilizer for trees, and nutrients for bacteria. At the zoo, the bones and pelt might be preserved as museum specimens, but the rest would be unceremoniously discarded along with gum wrappers and yesterday's leftovers.

No matter how special we are, I pondered, looking at our bear, our lives on this earth all face the same end. It is only our relationship with God and the impact we have on those we leave behind that will matter at the end.

God gave Solomon wisdom and very great insight, and a breadth of understanding as measureless as the sand on the seashore. He spoke about plant life, from the cedar of Lebanon to the hyssop that grows out of walls. He also spoke about animals and birds, reptiles, and fish. 1 Kings 4:29, 33

———◈———

I picture Solomon studying butterflies, fascinated with flowers, marvelling at a gecko, and enthralled with all that God had created. He would have loved pandas. But Solomon also noted that the wise, like the fool, will pass away. He said, "Like the fool, the wise too must die! In the same way rich men die and leave their inheritance to others." [Ecclesiastes 2:16 and Proverbs 13:22] So, if like the panda, we all end up dying, what's the point? At the end of Ecclesiastes, his famous treatise on the meaning of life, he says, "Now that all has been heard, here is the conclusion of the matter; fear God and keep his commandments, for this is the duty of all mankind." So regardless of where your body ends up, obeying God and having a relationship with him is, in the end, all that matters.

———◈———

Lord Jesus, thank you that because of you we have a future that is secure, and a present that is worth living for. Help us to enjoy this life, and make the most of it, but never to make this world our only focus. Help us to see it through the lens of eternity. As we walk through this life let us make your intangibles—love, grace, and relationship with you and others, primary. Remind us not to focus on riches, or our physical needs in this world. Help us to leave those things with you and trust you to provide what we need for each day. Jesus, thank you for reminding us that the flowers of the field grow even though they do not labor or spin. And that even Solomon in all his splendor was not dressed like one of them [Matthew 6:28,29]. Amen

On Keeping Things Sterile

Surgery? No. Too complicated!" That had been Dr. Lin's firm opinion shortly after I arrived at the zoo. I had inquired about surgery protocols and remembered the conversation clearly. I could still picture him waving his hand dismissively as he sank into his office chair and poured himself a thin green tea.

"If the animals need surgery, we take them to the Number Eight Peoples Hospital down the road and let them handle it."

I pictured myself walking a lion into the local hospital for a quick colonoscopy. In my mind it made for a busy day at the ER. The dear human doctors at the Number Eight People Hospital, for all of their skill, must also have been baffled by the peculiar anatomy of our patients. And all that hair. And the horns and fangs. Birds have air sacks behind their lungs, ruminants have four stomachs, and snakes, well, it's hard to find limbs for the ECG leads. So, to reduce their stress and improve patient outcomes, I had hoped to set up an appropriate surgery at the zoo hospital.

"We'd love to do surgery, but we don't have the equipment," Dr. Lin had continued. Then, leaning forward he had whispered, "And we don't have much experience, which makes us pretty nervous."

I could relate to the cold tightening of the stomach that grips surgeons before the first cut of a new procedure—the life on the cold steel table in your hands, while owners are anxiously wringing theirs in the waiting room. Many a surgeon has stared at the ceiling in the silence of the night, terrified of a challenging surgery looming with the dawn of the next day.

But even surgeons need to start somewhere, so I had planted the seeds of possibility.

"I have some experience with surgery, so I can help with that part, and the equipment"—I paused to think but came up empty—"maybe we can scrounge that up somehow."

That was months ago and I had let the topic rest as we adjusted to life in China. Now that my packages of hemostats, forceps, clamps, and scalpels had arrived, I was anxious to put them to use. We also had a rudimentary anesthetic set up, so the zoo officials felt it was time we started doing some of our own surgeries. "Makes the zoo look professional," they said.

"Now that we have the anaesthetic machine," I said to Dr. Lin, "all we need is a really clean room and some surgery packs."

These surgical packs consisted of scissors, clamps, and forceps that were set apart and kept only for one purpose: surgery. They had to be immaculate. No strands of hair or dried blood could be tolerated. Then they needed to be sterilized—removing any hidden impurity to be of use to a surgeon.

For several afternoons I carefully opened and shut the ratchet closures on all my instruments, scrutinizing them for loose joints. Scissors were put through their paces on dead animals to see if they would cleanly slice through muscle and tendons, and every set of forceps was held up to the light to see if their teeth meshed snuggly enough. Then I grouped them into suitable sets: a big chunky one, with lots of clamps for abdominal and bowel surgery; one with bone clamps and a wire saw for orthopedic procedures; and my favourite, a set with miniscule scissors, infinitesimal clamps, and whisper-thin suture for eye surgery.

Next, I found myself squeezing through the musty heat of a local fabric market, feeling bolts of cloth looking for a good tight weave.

"This one is a best seller," the saleslady said, pointing me to a playful dinosaur print. I decided on a boring army green, much to the disappointment of the saleslady. Smiling dinosaurs just didn't seem fitting for the professional look the zoo was going for.

Back at the office, Dr. Lin leaned over my desk inquisitively as I smoothed out the green squares and gently laid the select piles of instruments in the centre of each one. Then I opened a gauze pack, counted and recounted exactly ten pieces, balancing the snowy squares on each little hill, topping them off with a new scalpel blade. Lastly, I placed a little coloured cardboard at the foot of each set.

"What is that for?" Dr. Lin asked.

"That is for checking sterility. You see this dark circle? It changes colour when the inside of the pack gets hot enough to kill the bacteria."

Dr. Lin nodded appreciatively.

Finally, with a triumphant flourish, I folded and burrito-rolled each pack, securing it with heat-resistant tape and carried them to the conference room, setting them in a tidy pile on the middle of the table.

"How do you think we should sterilize them?" I asked the group that had gathered to witness the Canadian foreigner's latest antics.

"We could boil them," Dr. Yang suggested.

"And how would we dry them?" Dr. Wu asked.

"How about the microwave?"

"Wouldn't the metal spark and the cloth catch on fire?"

"What about an oven?"

"No, it would go up in flames!"

Thoughtful heads nodded as we pondered this dilemma when Tang Ya, our junior assistant, jumped up and darted out of the room, returning triumphantly with a large pressure cooker.

"This is from the back of the storage closet," he said. "It used to work, but the gauge broke and now I use it to hold old rags."

"Then we will buy a new one," Director Li decided resolutely, heading to her phone.

Two days later a shiny new pressure cooker, complete with a working gauge, appeared at the hospital. I was thrilled.

Dr. Lin and I immersed ourselves in the instruction book. This machine, with its submarine screw lid, was a bit cumbersome to use but had the advantage that if the power went out, you could still sterilize instruments by putting it over an open fire, a surprisingly thoughtful feature for a country where power outages were a regular occurrence. It was simple, but it would do the job. We added water to the inner chamber, loaded the instrument packs into the screen basket, lowered it into the machine, screwed down the lid, plugged it in, and waited.

Ten minutes later tiny satisfying wisps of steam curled from the valves.

"Once steam is seen, close the pressure valves," we read in the instruction book. Like obedient students we dutifully depressed the valve and sat back waiting for the next step. Then, for a very long time, nothing happened.

I sat, drumming my fingers on the table, looking at my watch, then at the pot, and then back at Dr. Lin. My foreign preoccupation with efficiency and time was becoming evident. Dr. Lin was much more accustomed to waiting and peacefully leaned back in his chair with Zen-like calm, gently easing over a page in his newspaper. He was the picture of tranquility. It was maddening.

Darn thing, I thought. *Is it even working?*

Impatiently, I crept up to the machine to check the pressure gauge, wondering if the needle had moved. I bent down and squinted at the dial, gently tapping it with my finger, completely unprepared for the looming onslaught when, like a live thing—*it attacked.*

Scalding blasts of steam screamed from all four sides of both safety valves, shooting a boiling fog into every corner of the room. Dr. Lin jumped, dropped his newspaper, and beat me out the door. Cautiously we peered around the corner to watch our machine vent its anger. Steam filled the tiny room as the cooker continued its fit of rage and disappeared behind a veil of boiling haze. Then, slowly, the shrieking lowered to an angry snarl, until the valves closed, and the steam subsided.

"The safety valve can keep the constant pressure," the English translation in the instruction book had said. It had not mentioned sudden blasts of scalding high-pressure steam barbequing unsuspecting bystanders. Our pressure cooker/sterilizer would require a delicate touch and a bold heart.

In the end, with our machine soothed and returned to its enclosure in the pharmacy, we returned to our neat pile of thoroughly cooked instrument packs. Reverently I placed them in the glass cupboard, adjusting them to show their best side. Dr. Lin put his arm around my shoulder and smiled, admiring our handiwork. There was a unique joy in having something so carefully set apart for special use.

Come out from them and be separate, says the Lord. 2 Cor. 6:17
But you are a chosen race, a royal priesthood, a holy nation, a people for
his own possession, that you may proclaim the excellencies of him who
called you out of darkness into his marvelous light.
1 Peter 2:9-10
Do you not know that your body is a temple of the Holy Spirit within you,
whom you have from God? 1 Cor. 6:19

———◉———

Holy is a misunderstood word. When God says something is holy, it means it is set apart, chosen, and purified for a special purpose—*his* purpose. In Exodus, God describes the tabernacle—the tent where he would dwell among his people—in astonishing detail because it was holy (set apart) for God and had to be perfect. You and I are the temple of the Holy Spirit—purified by Christ and set apart (made holy) to be used by God to share his love with a broken and diseased world. To use us in his quest to redeem mankind we, like surgical instruments, need to be purified and set apart so that when he calls on us, we are ready to dive into hard situations, malignant circumstances, and diseased hearts. And with each set of newly purified, holy instruments that God plucks out of the mire of this world, God smiles.

———◉———

Lord, in our modern world, "holiness" feels like a vestige of a bygone era. Help us to realize how special it is to be set apart by you, and for you. Help us to remember the cost you paid so that we could be made clean. Let us not look down on holiness as something old and stodgy, but as the pure radiance of your presence, fully alive in us. Cause us to crave that kind of life—a life set apart by you, for you, in which your light can freely shine. Lord, we want to be that royal priesthood that proclaims your excellencies and calls people out of darkness into your marvelous light. Fill us with your Spirit and make us holy we pray. Amen

Surgery and the Media

Small groups of fallow deer shuffled aimlessly about their cobble-stone enclosure as I sauntered past them on my morning rounds. Their numbers were healthy, but the animals were not. I zipped my coat to the collar, wrapped my arms around me to ward off the damp cold of late fall, and stopped to contemplate the herd. One lonely little fellow was leaning against a concrete wall and chewing listlessly on a potato chip bag. It was a welcome change in his mundane existence, but chewing on plastic bags also had a down-side.

Many of our deer had developed a taste for the empty snack bags, which visitors would toss into the enclosure. The dusting of flavour in the empty bags was just enough to captivate them. Anything was better than staring at a wall—even chip-dust. Bits of blue and yellow peaked out between his lips as he chewed. Finally, deciding it was more trouble than the effort was worth, he spit out the unsatisfying mass and stared at the disappointment at his feet.

Excellent decision, I thought.

He was one of the lucky ones. Two weeks earlier, we had done a post-mortem on his friend, who had starved to death with a belly full of knotted plastic bags.

As my eyes swept across the scene, I watched other, equally gaunt deer, drift about the paddock. My colleagues had also noticed the problem, and seeing as we now had a "professional surgery set-up," as the higher ups called it, it was decided that *preventative* surgeries would be a grand idea.

Plastic is not visible on x-ray so the only practical way we had to diagnose (or resolve) the problem was surgical. The plan was simple. Select a particularly thin animal, assume a tangle of plastic bags causing a blockage in the rumen, the big fermenting stomach, and do a rumenotomy. To do this, the large fermenting stomach of a cow or deer is opened, allowing the surgeon to look inside and remove any nasty trespassers; bales of plastic bags, tangles of wire, chewed up welcome mats. Anything really that did not pass on its own and was causing a problem.

The plan was admirable, but I was concerned. Our anesthetic machine was only designed for small animals under twenty pounds. Even our scrawniest patient would tip the scale at twice that.

"We are going to have our surgery broadcast on TV," Dr. Lin said excitedly as he walked toward me in the hall of the hospital. "Director Tong has invited the media to witness our surgery. Isn't that exciting?"

I stared at him.

"Is it?" I asked. "I mean, is that really a good idea? We have not tested our set-up. We don't know if the surgery will succeed. We haven't done one of these before. And it's a lot of pressure to do this for the first time in front of the cameras."

"Oh, I'm not worried. We'll be fine. After all, we have you!" Dr. Lin beamed confidently as he spun around and scurried off to the cafeteria. My concerns were not worth being late for lunch.

The following day, as my colleagues busied themselves in the treatment room, wiping walls and glass shelves to a camera-ready sparkle and setting up a makeshift surgery table, I felt it necessary to voice my apprehensions more clearly.

Dr. Li stood in the middle of the room in her chic dress and stiletto heels and directed the cleanup, keeping up a cheerful banter with the staff about the great surgery ahead. Everything was rainbows and butterflies—and I was a dark cloud entering the sunny little scene.

"I am worried!" I said pleadingly, resisting the urge to wring my hands and stamp my feet. "Our anesthetic set up is not suitable for an animal of this size."

No one seemed concerned.

"And what if there is no plastic in the rumen of the deer we pick? How would that look to the media?"

My second volley was met with happy smiles and nods. The cheery wiping of shelves continued. I was getting nowhere, so, needing to do something more dramatic, I played my trump card, expecting it to stop everyone mid-wipe as they envisioned the catastrophe to come.

"And what if the deer dies during surgery?" I said, searching their faces one by one. "Wouldn't that be a terrible loss of face?!?"

My ace was met with placating nods and smiles that said, "Poor foreigner, he just doesn't get it."

"I understand that you are concerned Dr. Paul, but the news media and TV crews have already been arranged, and so, as you can see, we have no choice but to go ahead," Dr. Li said tenderly. It felt like she was about to hand me a lollipop and shoo me outside to play.

I didn't see. And there was still a choice. And my face showed it, so Dr. Li continued. "Really. Don't be concerned. *You* do the surgery, and *we* will take care of the anesthesia."

I raised an eyebrow.

"Really," she repeated. "It will be just fine. No need to worry."

Then she gave me a last reassuring nod and turned to point someone to a portion of shelf that needed a little more polishing.

But I did worry—a lot. And driven by fear of what *could* happen, I prepared for every nightmare scenario I could think of. Visions of a blue-tongued deer gasping for air had me check and recheck the oxygen tank. Images of fermenting rumen juice spilling into the open abdomen made me double up on sterile gauze squares. Vomiting under anesthesia made a disturbing appearance, but having no extra-long breathing tubes suitable to intubate the long narrow face of a deer, I suppressed that image and continued setting up.

I was wiping a corner of the room that had not seen love for many years when my colleagues eased a fancy new machine into the treatment room. "Zhuan Ye (professional) ECG" it said in shiny silver lettering. The zoo had purchased it just for this occasion. It came complete with a digital read-out and a blood-oxygen meter and was an admirably modern touch to our makeshift operating theater. But sadly, it did not allay my fears. Used correctly, it could give us moment by moment reports about our patient; however, we had no way of correcting a problem should it arise. It would either be a soothing voice, calming us with gentle whispers as it beeped "all is well" to the steady beat of a healthy heart, or it would be a terrifying alarm screaming "Death is imminent!" as the heart slowed and we helplessly watched the animal gasp for air.

I finished setting up my instruments, straightened the plywood board on the desk that would serve as our surgery table, and took a deep breath. The next day would be a big one.

Next morning, I kissed the kids, as they blissfully munched on their cornflakes and sipped their chocolate milk. Michelle gave me an extra hug and whispered, "You've got this," as I headed out the door.

Stepping out of the van, I made my way through a small crowd of cameramen and reporters milling about the entrance of the hospital and looked for Dr. Lin.

"He is at the deer enclosure darting one of the deer," Dr. Yang whispered in his gentle librarian voice.

I walked to our makeshift surgery and did a last mental check of what lay ahead. Looking around, I nodded quietly to myself. The floor was freshly swept, the glass shelves sparkled, and the anaesthetic and "signs of life" machine were seated at the head of the surgery table waiting for the deer to be served. Satisfied that we were as prepared as we could be, I reached for the hair clippers and headed to the storage room to look for an extension cord. At least we could do the shaving outdoors and keep the hair out of the surgery.

I was standing at the ready at the hospital entrance when a banged-up wheel barrow came down the path, pushed by two cheerful deer keepers. A head wobbled over the edge of one side and four legs stuck out like french-fries from a snack box. It was an unimpressive entrance, but even so, a gaggle of reporters and cameras swarmed toward the arriving patient.

Gently, we laid the deer on the steps outside the hospital and got to work. The cameras clicked as we clipped and shaved. Then we carried it inside and laid it on the plywood table. Except for the plywood, the room looked impressive. Everyone was dressed in masks and pale-blue surgical gowns, including the maintenance staff who had assembled to enjoy the spectacle. We looked like an immense surgical team. The ECG and anesthetic machine were connected to the deer and two rows of reporters settled around us—the first row edging close to the table, the second row standing on stools and peering over their colleagues to get a better camera angle.

I opened the surgical pack, placed a new scalpel on the handle, and stood over our patient like a conductor, with a scalpel in one hand and a gauze square in the other. The room hushed in anticipation.

"Make a bold incision," our surgery professor had admonished us as students. Camera flashes lit up the surgery site as I made my first cut, slicing cleanly through the skin in a long straight line. Blood oozed slowly from the two skin edges as they separated. I dabbed them with gauze (too much blood might offend the viewers). It had been a long time since I had done any surgery, but the scalpel rested comfortably in my hand. I looked up at the cameras, and for the first time in several days, I felt good.

As foreigners in China, we often felt like buffoons, bumbling about and struggling with even the most mundane tasks. Speaking Chinese allowed us to putter along quite nicely if there were no complications, but when problems arose, our vocabulary went out the window and we were once again reduced to blabbering fools. Sending letters, making phone calls, even ordering food at a restaurant could be formidable tasks, and our egos were regularly taken to the mat and given a good pummeling. I was hoping that today was not going to be one of those days.

The camera crews faded into the background as I became increasingly absorbed in my task. "Cut through the muscle layers; enter the abdomen; locate the rumen; then suture it to the skin with non-penetrating bites to secure it and seal it away from the rest of the abdomen."

The rumen is a fermentation vat and is filled with partly digested grass and heaps of bacteria that are busy breaking down the juicy soup. Therefore, we had arranged ahead of time that once I had the rumen secured, Dr. Lin would step forward, incise the organ, and examine the inside of the rumen as I stood back, hands clasped carefully in front of me to maintain sterility. He would dramatically plunge his hand in, pull out the plastic bags, hold them aloft for the audience to see, and I would then step back in to close. Easy-peezy.

I watched with anticipation as Dr. Lin incised the rumen and reached in. At first, all he produced were handfuls of sloppy, digested grass. The room filled with the sweet smell of fermented greenery as he slowly filled the metal pail Tang Ya was holding at his side. It was disappointing, but not unexpected. Rumens *should* have grass, but my stomach tightened as the handfuls got smaller and less impressive. Dr. Lin's eyes narrowed as he reached in past his elbow, probing about inside. Everyone waited for the big reveal. Long seconds passed, his forehead wrinkled, and even with his surgical mask could not hide his deepening concern. His eyes looked back at me anxiously. Nothing! No plastic, no bags—nothing!

Director Li stepped forward, an elegant crimson lace dress and high-heeled shoes peeking out from under her plain blue surgical gown. She smiled. The reporters smiled back as she chatted with them. Her calm control put everyone at ease, and it seemed inevitable that she would make it all better as she donned a mask and gloves and reached inside. Slowly and methodically, she inspected every recess of the now empty rumen, hoping for a shred of plastic, a twist tie, a rubber band, anything that could justify our surgical hullabaloo. Nothing. Just a few last stubborn bits of hay. Then with all the grace of a movie star stepping off the red carpet she nodded to me and then to the reporters. Tang Ya dutifully scooped rumen contents back into the animal's stomach, and I stepped forward to rinse the site, close the rumen, and finish the surgery. Director Tong led the reporters into the hall. *What would he say?* I wondered as I closed the first muscle layer, glad that I was not the director of a zoo. *What would I say?* I suddenly sweat as I closed the second layer, realizing that as the foreign expert, they would want an "expert opinion." Such a fuss and no results. It would be awkward. My "expert opinion" had been that we should not do the surgery. But I couldn't say that. I contemplated my options. Running away seemed easiest, but I decided against it. I carefully finished the skin sutures, making sure it looked extra neat and professional, like a perfect bow on an ugly present.

"So how do you feel about today's surgery Dr. Paul?" the reporter asked as I stepped into the hall, untying my gown.

The virus I had been fighting was making itself obvious as I wiped my forehead with my mask. The stress of surgery was working in its favour. My ears were plugged, my brain was wet cotton, and my nose was stuffed.

"The procedure was diagnostic," I mumbled stuffily.

"Many deer that have already died were found to have plastic bag obstructions in their gut on post mortem. This was the primary suspicion for this deer. Surgery was the only way to know if that was the case here."

Unfortunately, in this *particular* case, in front of the cameras, it was not.

The TV and newspaper crews slowly drifted back to their cars, and we lifted the deer to a recovery pen. He seemed small, cold, and alone. I was concerned. Others stood beside it, watching it recover. Finally, as the last reporter left, Dr. Lin took a deep, well-deserved breath. We walked back into the surgery. It looked like a war zone.

Groggily, I started to bundle up stained drapes and bloody gauze squares when I heard a commotion in the hall. I dropped the drapes and ran to the deer. It lay stiffly outstretched on the concrete, gasping for air, and paddling in convulsions. I had arrived just in time to watch as it struggled, shuddered, and died. We stood in stunned silence. The deer had been too weak, too cold, and too run-down before surgery. Surgery and an inadequate oxygen supply during anesthetic was the crushing blow.

The next day a few reporters came back and asked about the deer. The mild cold that had started in my chest the day of the surgery was now a full-blown infirmity. They interviewed us in turn and finally turned to me, hoping for some quotable tidbit from the foreigner.

"Unfortunately, he didn't make it," I snuffled, staring at the floor. There was not much else to say. Sometimes things just don't work out the way you hoped.

Do not set foot on the path of the wicked or walk in the way of evildoers. Avoid it, do not travel on it; turn from it and go on your way. Proverbs 4:15-16

———◉———

Sin is a lot like a plastic chip bag. It tempts us with a whisper of sugar or tugs at our craving for salt, but it will kill us. "Not ideal," we convince ourselves as we consume just a little taste. "But no real harm done." Over time, the consumption of sin gets easier. We crave the instant high it offers and hush the warnings of the Spirit. And by the time we recognize the devastating effect it's having, we are too addicted to let go. Like a cruel indigestible, ball of plastic in our gut, the sin churns away, making us ever sicker, refusing to be spit up. The great physician can heal us, but the damage sin does to us and those around us can leave some nasty scars. God wants us to avoid that pain, so he warns us to flee from sin. But if we do find ourselves with our belly full of plastic—the great physician makes house calls.

———◉———

Lord Jesus, forgive us for so easily being led away by sinful desires. For craving a fleeting hint of sin more than the everlasting joy of your company. Lord, thank you that you do not hold our foolishness against us. Thank you for your patience even in the midst of open rebellion. Lord, block our path if we start to wander in the direction of evil. Keep us pure and set apart, so that we honour you with our lives. Lord, you have warned us that "Everyone who practices sin is a slave to sin." (John 8:34) But you also gave us the promise that "The slave does not remain in the house forever; the son remains forever. So if the Son sets you free, you will be free indeed." (John 8:35,36) So if we do find ourselves caught in the web, and are enslaved by sin, free us. We have only one hope Jesus—and it is you! So it is in your name that we pray. Amen.

Christmas Surprise

You are doing a great job," I said as James piled one more ornamental trinket on the sagging tree branch. I put my arm around Michelle as we watched our kids, carefully choosing each little treasure and then reaching as high as they could to place it just right. When all the ornament cartons were empty, they stood back and admired the tree, the bottom half of the which was now festooned in Christmas cheer.

The bright lights of the Christmas tree lit the scene—including, frustratingly, a stack of moving boxes stubbornly hugging the corner of the room just beyond the tree.

Unpacking in a new home, I discovered, happens in stages. First, great joy as boxes are opened and the first long-awaited goodies see the light of day. Then, chaos sets in as rooms get overrun with half-empty boxes and random things searching for a permanent home. Gradually, the cartons empty completely, and the jumbled chaos is replaced by order. You end up with a few boxes of miscellaneous stuff. These are the rebel boxes—the ones that hold the collection of arbitrary knickknacks and remain defiantly stacked in hidden corners. They are usually left to their own devices until the next move.

We had reached this final stage not long before Christmas. Michelle had done a remarkable job of setting up home. The tree was up, the house was cozy, and only those few last stubborn boxes remained resistant to her efforts.

Long before we had landed in China, we had planned to invite the whole veterinary staff to our house for a Christmas dinner. I remember closing my eyes to picture the scene as we lay in bed, months before leaving.

"And we'll have turkey, and stuffing, and pie and all the trimmings," Michelle mused as we imagined the festive event.

"The smell of gingerbread will greet our guests at the door. The tree will be glittering, casting shadows in the warm glow of Christmas candles, soft carols will be playing, and after a wonderful meal the kids will put on their pajamas and snuggle up with our new friends as we read them all the Christmas story."

It was a peaceful, Rockwellian scene, and I drifted off to sleep to the soft glimmer of Christmas candles.

It's funny how much reality can differ from imagination.

Twenty-two giddy guests arrived at our house for Christmas dinner. All five vets, several support staff, all of their spouses, and numerous children (some of whom were not related to any of the adults) had come to the foreigner's house for Christmas. It was their opportunity to see if Christmas movie scenes lived up to the hype, and we were determined to prove that they did.

"Honey, with that big of a crowd, how about a big pot of spaghetti?" I suggested to Michelle.

"No, I just can't do that. It just wouldn't feel right. And anyway, we have lots of time to prepare," she said, turning around to stir the pot of pig fat rendering on the stove. Pie crust, she informed me, needed lard to have that delicate flakiness. I loved her determination to make it an authentic experience.

In Canada, where ingredients are readily available—where lard comes in cans and turkeys come frozen—preparing a full sit-down Christmas dinner is a big task. But in China, it rose to a whole new level of complicated. The turkey had to be special ordered from Shanghai and many trimmings ferreted out or, like the lard bubbling for hours on the stove, had to be created.

Dinner was planned for Saturday evening, and so, on Monday, Michelle started to prepare. There was a lot to do, but we seemed to have enough time to get it all done. We would have a week to get ready for the zoo meal event, then a week to recover and prepare for two more Christmas events: a meal with neighbours and our own family celebration, which would include several guests. We would honour Jesus by celebrating his birth with friends and family, *and* share his story with thirty or so new acquaintances. It was a solid, two-week plan.

But God—watching our carefully organized preparations—had other plans.

· Monday: Michelle starts cooking. Rachel gets a cold and stays home.

· Tuesday: Rachel is still home. In the evening we all pile into the van and drive to the kids' Christmas concert in the south end of the city.

· Wednesday: Rachel feels better and returns to school. Isaac is sick and stays home.

· Thursday: Isaac returns to school. James starts vomiting. We discover that he has vomited in his bed at night. We change and wash the blankets, sheets, and foam mattress.

I get to work late. James vomits all day long. Isaac comes home, gets diarrhea, and vomits in bed. We wash more sheets and blankets.

· Friday: James is still vomiting. Both Isaac and James are weak. Michelle continues to unpack and prepare for the meal on Saturday.

· Saturday morning of the Christmas vet dinner: We take the kids downtown to practice their Sunday morning Christmas pageant. Luke announces he feels ill and doesn't eat for the rest of the day. Michelle cooks, and we prepare the seating for the guests.

· Saturday afternoon: We finish setting up and cooking. James, Luke, and Isaac still do not eat all day (James has not eaten in three days). At six, the guests arrive. The meal is a success. We explain Christmas and have Director Li read the Christmas account from the Bible in Chinese. For most, it is the first time they have ever heard it—or any portion of the Bible. Between the meal and dessert, James vomits on the kitchen floor. Michelle cleans it up and serves dessert without anyone noticing. The guests leave, and we clean up.

· Sunday: Church Christmas pageant in the morning, then home to finish cleaning up from the night before.

· Monday: Isaac has diarrhea. We are concerned because, as a paraplegic, he dehydrates quickly.

· Tuesday: All the kids are home sick. James wakes up with croup. He barks and coughs all day.

· Tuesday night: James's croup gets worse. I am at work preparing for the aforementioned deer surgery. I get directions to a human hospital before I leave work just in case we need to take James there. At night, James sleeps with us in our bed so we can keep an eye on him.

· Wednesday: The day of the deer surgery and media frenzy. I get sick myself (a cold).

· Thursday: Rachel wakes up vomiting. More sheets and bedding to wash. She vomits all day—every fifteen minutes, like clockwork. Michelle can get nothing done. My cold is worse. Michelle is at her wit's end. I go to work late to meet with media following the deer debacle.

· Thursday: Rachel is still ill but vomiting less. In the evening we take the kids Christmas shopping so that they can buy presents for each other. No one is healthy but we have no other option.

· Friday: I take the day off work. We take Luke to a friend's house. We try to book flights for a much-needed break over Chinese New Year. We have not seen the sun in over a month and hope to escape to somewhere warm. That evening, as I return from downtown, the zoo calls. The giraffe is giving birth! It could be an all-night affair. Michelle and the kids (in their pajamas) join me in going to the zoo. We get to see the birth, but the baby has a hard time standing up. Michelle takes the kids home, and I stay until ten-thirty. That night we wrap Christmas presents, but I do not sleep much, knowing that the baby giraffe is not doing well.

· Saturday: The giraffe baby is standing and drinking. We are relieved. Michelle starts to feel ill, but none-the-less starts to prepare another Christmas dinner. We have invited four single ladies to join us for Christmas on Sunday. We clean the house. A TV crew wants to come and do a segment on Christmas with a foreign family. We cannot pass up the opportunity. They spend three hours at our house. Rachel is exhausted and sick and just wants to sleep. The TV crew asks that she not be in the shots as she does not look "happy." We share the meaning of Christmas and sing Christmas carols for the cameras. The piece is to be shown on provincial TV. The camera crew leaves. Michelle prepares supper because our neighbours are coming over for dinner.

· Sunday: It's Christmas! We do not go to the fellowship church service in the morning. Rachel is still too sick, and we are too drained. Two single teachers from the international school and a young researcher from the panda base come for Christmas dinner in the afternoon. They miss home.

· Monday: I take a day off work, and we try to recover.

That night we fell into bed, exhausted but amazed. It had been a long and draining Christmas. But by God's grace, and through his strength, we have made it through and shared the story of his love with family, friends, coworkers, neighbours... and over *200 million people* through a TV program! It was more than we could think or imagine, but it certainly is not how we would have planned it!

Now to him who is able to do immeasurably more than all we ask or imagine, according to his power that is at work within us, to him be glory in the church and in Christ Jesus throughout all generations, for ever and ever! Amen. Eph. 6:20,21
You intended to harm me, but God intended it for good to accomplish what is now being done, the saving of many lives. Gen. 50:20

———— ◉ ————

We want God to use us in mighty ways, and we are happy to offer him suggestions of how best to do that. Those suggestions almost never include adding trials or struggles to our lives. But God's goal is not our ease, or our success (at least not how we usually define it). His goal is to give us the greatest gift he can: himself. God has our ultimate good at heart, so sometimes he allows challenges in our lives to draw us to himself. We don't usually welcome these trials, but amazingly he uses even these struggles and trials to do more than anything we could think or imagine. He loves taking what looks hopeless and turning it into a triumph. Just look at the cross, the tomb, and the empty grave.

———— ◉ ————

Heavenly Father, forgive us for the arrogance of assuming that we know what is good for us better than you do. Forgive us for thinking that when you allow difficulty in our lives, you love us less. Your love for us was proven on the cross. Help us to cling to that reality. Lord use our lives, with all its messy situations, to draw us to you and to make you famous. Help us to realize that when we yield our will and our way to your perfect will and way, you can do immeasurably more than we could ever think or imagine. Lord, help us to trust you completely. For your glory's sake we pray. Amen

Reptiles and Winter

Chengdu was not famous for its weather. *Clouds* was the most common picture on Rachel's kindergarten weatherboard. Most days were grey and overcast. Summer rain usually fell in a misty drizzle, and in the winter, heavy blankets of fog shrouded the city. Slate-grey skies were so normal and the moon so rarely seen that the locals had a saying, "The dogs of Chengdu bark at the moon."

Oddly, these same locals also took pride in the terrific weather of their city. It was never as glacial as the cities on the border of Russia, and not as sweltering as the far south. To us, the steamy thirty-some degrees of summer was plenty hot, but it was the winters that assaulted us most—which was hard—because as hearty Canadians, we wore our tolerance of cold weather with national pride.

As the summer heat cooled, my friends at the zoo would ask me about seasons and weather in Canada.

"Yes, it can get a bit nippy where we live in Canada," I would say, hiding my pride with appropriate Canadian humility—and then subtly mention the minus twenty degrees we often saw in the dead of winter. Eyes would widen, eyebrows would rise, mouths would hang open, and someone would whisper, "Aayahhh!"

Then everyone would assure me that I would have no issue with winter in Chengdu. It would be a cinch compared to Canada.

They were wrong.

Winter in Chengdu was entirely different. Canadian winters are cold, dry, and the sun that shines in the azure sky lights the glittering white world in diamonds. Indoors, flames dance in our wood stove and keep our fingers and toes warm and cozy. That represented winter for us.

In Chengdu, the relentless damp drove the inescapable cold through the many layers of wool and long-johns, through the skin, and deep into the bones. The grey concrete homes were not insulated, doors were poorly fitted, and the windows single-paned and drafty. Indoor temperatures were not much different from outside. When the thermometer dipped to three misty degrees outside, the nine damp degrees inside did little to warm the toes. Frosty toilet seats were a shock to the hindquarters, and frigid bed sheets sucked the heat from your body as you slipped, stiff and corpse-like, under the covers. We wore long-johns and parkas indoors. It was not fashionable, but it was warmer.

For us warm-blooded creatures, with the option of downy clothes and space heaters, this winter assault was an inconvenience. But for the cold-blooded reptiles at the zoo, it was the difference between life and death, and we were losing them at a rapid pace as the winter progressed.

I surveyed the latest casualty from the reptile house as it lay, long and stiff, on the white tiles of the autopsy table. Steadying the lifeless body, I placed my scalpel on its belly and made an incision to inspect the internal organs and determine the cause of death, but it was more of a confirmation than detective work. Regardless of the final blow, the underlying issue was the same. It was too cold. This left their immune systems weak and ineffective. Appetites were suppressed, mild infections were able to run rampant, and the whole long slender body just didn't function as it was designed. The snake keeper stood beside me, hands in his pockets, watching the gloomy proceedings.

"This is depressing," was all he said.

I nodded and, as a reptile lover myself, decided I needed to do something about it.

Returning to my desk I flipped open my laptop and started tapping the keys, searching the internet to learn about each species. Some of our snakes were elegant, slender tree dwellers with a preferred diet of birds or lizards. Others came from tropical swamps and liked fish and frogs, and some enjoyed a long winter nap in a cool hollow. In order to keep each animal healthy, we would need to recreate a more native environment, including the right heat, moisture, and preferred food. As the only member of the team who could research things on English web sites, it was my task to ferret out the needed information.

For some of our reptiles, this worked well. Rat and king snakes were commonly kept as pets, so detailed care sheets were readily available. Care of crocodiles and alligators was harder to come by, but commercial farms had a fair bit of information. Then I typed "Cobra Care" into the search engine.

A list of spine-chilling articles appeared—accompanied by graphic images. "*Care* for a *cobra* bite victim"; "Intensive *care* after *cobra* attack"; "*Cobra* bite intensive *care* bill hits $100,000." It made for riveting reading.

Sobered by vivid pictures of swollen limbs, blue lips, and ghastly necrotic wounds, I returned to the reptile house. Meimei (little sister), our two-meter-long king cobra, stared at me. "The bite from a large one could kill an elephant," the website had said. Fortunately, our girl was only average size, but then, I was no elephant. The trick for our reptiles, I realized, was to provide medical care for them, without needing it ourselves.

"I think the key to keeping our reptiles healthy is not more drugs but giving them an environment in which they can really thrive," I said to my colleagues during break, "because many come from warm climates."

But they didn't look up from their flip-phones and newspapers. Cold reptiles, it seemed, were not very engaging.

What we needed was "proof of concept."

I zipped up my fluffy down jacket, stuffed my hands in my pockets, and marched through the misty fog to the reptile house.

The doors were open, and the chill of the grey concrete walls did nothing to warm the atmosphere of the building.

"Our giant Malaysian River Turtle is not eating," the young keeper said, watching his charge and pursing his lips. "She doesn't even want the fish she usually loves."

At over thirty kilos, our turtle was an impressive animal, and seeing her floating, cold and listless in the concrete pool as the water slowly spun her around in circles, was a sad sight.

I rubbed my chin. "Well," I said, "she is from Malaysia, a *very* hot place. She'd probably enjoy a warmer bath."

"Yeah, but we don't have a heater," he said. "And I don't think the zoo will buy one."

"Why not?"

"Too expensive—water heaters for pools have pumps and stuff; and need to be professionally installed." He dug his hands deeper into his pockets and walked away.

I kept watching her float on the surface—spread-eagled and stiff. *There has to be a way*, I thought.

After lunch, I went for a walk. The long lunches at the zoo allowed for free time for exercise or exploration—and it was too cold in my office to just sit there.

Out on the street, I flowed along with the bustle of heavily quilted pedestrians and bundled up bicyclists, weaving and bobbing around street vendors who had spread their wares on the sidewalk. Shoelaces, combs, cheap canvas shoes, and other household bargains were on offer, displayed on the sidewalk in tidy piles. I stepped around one, noticed an odd contraption and squatted down.

"You have a keen eye," the vendor said. "That's a best seller. Good quality. You will love it. Heats tea really fast."

It was a simple device. A coil of heavy copper attached to a long electric cord. No buttons, no switches, no bells or whistles. Just a metal coil—attached to electricity.

"For you my friend—special price," he beamed, patting me on the shoulder. "Two dollars."

I nodded thoughtfully, handed him the money, and stuffed my prize into a pocket. "Simple, elegant and cheap," I thought.

Back at the reptile house I presented my find to the young keeper.

"What do you think?"

"Could work. How do you turn it on?"

"Just plug it in."

"No buttons?"

"No buttons."

"How much?"

"Two bucks. My treat."

"Hmmm," he said, weighing the heater in his hands.

I noticed him inspecting the cord.

"As long as we can set it up safely, there should be no problem," I said.

He pursed his lips and tilted his head as if he were about to decline. I leaned forward to say more, but in the end, he looked up and just nodded. He was a reptile keeper. They don't talk much.

An hour later we were inspecting our handiwork. The electric cord was safely hidden under a patio stone and disappeared under the man-gate of the enclosure. The other end—the copper coil—was tucked behind a large pile of rocks under the water in the corner of the pool. For such a large pool, in these temperatures, I was not worried about too much heat—not enough was more the issue.

"Not sure it will make much of a difference," the keeper said.

I nodded, but I was hopeful.

For the next while, every day, I dropped by the reptile house on my walks around the zoo. Every day I popped my head into the keepers' quarters, looking for my young friend. Every day he sat glumly, deep into the sports section of his newspaper.

"Any change?"

"Nope."

"Nothing?"

"Nope."

It was not encouraging, and he did little to elevate my spirits.

Over the next several days, hope gave way to resignation. I stopped looking forward to these meetings, so it was easy to think of walking *past* the reptile house on my way to lunch a week later. After all, I was hungry—and the meetings were deflating. But maybe, just maybe...

I popped my head through the door.

The young keeper put down his paper and smiled.

"She ate!"

"Seriously?"

"Yup, chomped up a whole fish. And she's moving a lot more."

We walked to see our big girl. She was relaxed—slowly paddling around the pool, poking into corners, and exploring her home. I watched her, marveling at the change. In the environment she was designed for, she was a spectacular creature—and she was happy.

I walked to the cafeteria smiling. All she had wanted was a bit of warm water. In her element she could thrive; away from it, she struggled, which is true for all animals. Trout prefer icy mountain streams. Tube worms do best at the bottom of deep-sea trenches, under the crush of miles of water, saddled up to a scalding thermal vent. And our river turtle—she was not a creature of extremes— she preferred the tepid waters of a shaded jungle. Each animal doing best in the environment it was designed for.

He is before all things, and in him all things hold together. Col. 1:17
For in him we live and move and have our being. Acts 17:28
I am the vine; you are the branches. If you remain in me and I in you,
you will bear much fruit; apart from me you can do nothing.
John 15:5
You make known to me the path of life; you will fill me with joy in your
presence, with eternal pleasures at your right hand. Psalm 16:11

———————◉———————

It is no secret that this world is in rough shape. Mental illness is on the rise; extremism and hatred are rampant; wars and conflicts are everywhere; and love, mercy and grace are in short supply around the globe. There is not one country or society where everything is rainbows and butterflies. It's almost as if we humans are missing something. Some vital ingredient in our lives without which we, and the societies we live in, just don't function right. Ever since humans rejected the rule of God and decided to go his or her own way, life has been fraught with problems. God created us to function perfectly, and beautifully, in the light of his presence. Without him, everything kind of falls apart.

———————◉———————

Heavenly Father, as we look at the world around us, we repent on behalf of ourselves and all humanity for rejecting you, and then being angry when life without you falls apart. We go our own way, reject your love and guidance, and then wonder why without you, the one who holds the world together, things don't work. Lord, help us be so connected to you, the true vine, that we are constantly sustained by your presence. We want to bear fruit, the fruit that comes from you: love, joy, peace, patience, kindness, goodness, faithfulness, gentleness, and self-control. Make known to us the paths of life and fill us with joy in your presence. Amen.

Anna

Anna lay, cold and lonely, on the concrete floor of her enclosure. At twenty-five, she was an elderly chimp but was usually quite healthy. Seeing as food was one of her only joys, the uneaten banana lying beside her shivering body was an ominous sign.

Anna was *not* one of our more endearing residents. She had no companions and little in her cage to amuse her, so she had regressed to a life of resentment, anger, and suspicion, filling her days throwing poo and spitting at passersby. She was tough and bitter and quite happy to cement her persona by smoking cigarettes, which she bummed off the keepers. Anna was a hard-bitten reprobate, but seeing her lying there, listless and alone, my heart went out to her.

"What do you think?" Dr. Lin asked.

"Let's start by anaesthetizing her to do a physical," I said.

"Hmmm. Can't do that, I'm afraid."

"Why not?"

"We are low on ketamine."

I had forgotten about the shortage. Ketamine is a potent anaesthetic, but it could be abused as a recreational drug, so it was highly controlled and available only in very limited quantities—or not at all—which was a problem.

Chimps are impressively strong with huge teeth, and, given Anna's gangster personality, none of us were willing to enter her cage without the chemical restraint that ketamine would offer. Dr. Lin leaned forward.

"We could try just injecting her with antibiotics," he said.

It was a reasonable option. We didn't know what was wrong with her and couldn't do a physical exam, but a bacterial infection was a distinct possibility so broad-spectrum antibiotics made sense as a first step. Anna was far too clever for us to sneak a pill into her food, so injectable antibiotics were the only option.

Anna, like all of our primates, was fast and intelligent and had become extremely adept at avoiding darts, racing to the far end of the enclosure and swaying wildly when she saw the blow tube, making her a very challenging target. But in her weakened state, she took no notice as Dr. Lin loaded a dart and quietly slipped the blow tube through the bars of the cage.

The next morning we gathered at the chimp exhibit and observed the sad, shivering heap of black fur that was Anna. She was noticeably worse.

"We can't let this go on," Director Li said resolutely. "Tang Ya, get the ketamine."

Tang Ya bounded out of the primate house and returned from the pharmacy moments later, bearing the last precious vial of anaesthetic in both hands. Cautiously, Dr. Lin loaded one of our imported darts with six milliliters of the precious liquid and slid it into our fancy dart gun. It was not a time to take chances.

Anna had seen the silver tube before and climbed up onto her bars. Shaking with fear and weakness, she screamed. Even in her feeble state, she was not going to make it easy. Losing that much ketamine would be a significant loss to the hospital. Dr. Lin hid the gun at his side and strolled casually down the hall, apparently going for an early lunch. Anna leaned forward to watch him walk away.

Director Li waved me over to the other side of the cage where the others had congregated. She handed a blow tube to Dr. Wu, our tallest and most imposing vet, who made a show of lowering it through the bars of the cage for Anna to see. The rest of the team yelled and waved their arms. I was a bit confused, but didn't want to feel left out, so I joined in, jumping around and yelling in English.

Anna raised her eyebrows and barked.

From the corner of my eye, I noticed Dr. Lin, slinking back and setting up in the far corner of the exhibit.

Moments later, Anna squealed, yanked the dart out of her rump and hurled it back at Dr. Lin, bouncing it off the bars of the cage in front of his face. She glared at him, but her anger was short-lived, and, as the drugs took hold, she relaxed.

"Will she fall?" Tang Ya wondered aloud, but Anna swung her tired self down and sauntered awkwardly to the back corner of her pen, folding up in a cozy, snoozing heap.

Cautiously, we entered the cage and rolled Anna onto her back. She was impressive. Her barrel chest and muscular arms could easily swing her hundred-pound body around the enclosure and her teeth rivaled some of the big cats. I inserted a thermometer into her back end. Thirty-four point five degrees. *That can't be right*, I thought, *that is much too low*. I shook the thermometer violently and reinserted it, almost disappearing it into her rear. Thirty-four point five degrees. Anna was in trouble.

"Let's take a blood sample and start with antibiotics and IV fluids for dehydration," Director Li suggested. Tang Ya was sent scampering to the hospital pharmacy and returned with bags of fluids and a bottle of antibiotic.

After her treatment, we went out for noodles, and Anna was allowed to wake up. By the afternoon, she was noticeably brighter and showed much greater spirit in avoiding the dart. I was pleased.

The next morning, we went back to see her, and Dr. Lin once again set up with the blow dart and approached the cage. Anna had enough of darts and made her feelings known. She swung up to her bars and gesticulated wildly, rocking back and forth and shrieking like a madwoman. Dr. Lin looked at us and shook his head. Darting was not an option. We needed to outsmart our quarry.

The primate keepers showed their value in the whole endeavour and enticed her within range by offering her a drink of chocolate milk, which was, next to smoking, one of her favourite treats. Anna knew a good thing when she saw it and warily inched over to have the treat poured into her mouth, suspiciously glancing sideways at Dr. Lin, who was casually leaning against the wall until, with surprising speed, he spun around. But Anna was smart. Before he had a chance to shoot, she swung up to a nearby perch, leaned forward, and glared angrily, not moving or screaming. *Why is she just sitting there?* I wondered. *Is she challenging him?* Dr. Lin, pleased that she was co-operating so nicely, set up and aimed for her thigh when a torrent of chocolate milk came raining down. Anna, too, could shoot things through the bars of the cage, and having unloaded her ammunition, she bounced up and down barking and grinning as she celebrated her brilliant revenge. Wet, sticky, and no longer having any fun, Dr. Lin retreated.

"Would she let me do it by hand?" I asked cautiously. "I could try to get her to the bars and use a fine needle."

"Oh, I don't think so," Director Li replied. "She won't let you get close, and if she does, she might try to grab you."

"Could I try?" I asked. "Anna doesn't know me, or fear me, and I don't look like the others here who have injected her over the years."

Director Li nodded reluctantly. "Fine, but be careful! I don't want you losing a finger."

I filled a syringe with antibiotic, attached the thinnest needle we had, and approached the cage to chat with Anna. I spoke in English. We were both foreigners in China, and I wanted to strike a friendly "fellow-immigrant-in-a-strange-land" kind of tone. Everyone watched.

Anna responded by hooting gently and swinging down from her bars. Cautiously she approached, sat down, and stuck her hand out through the bars of the cage. I stroked the back of her leathery black fingers. Anna looked up and hooted softly. I showed her the syringe and needle.

"It's okay, girl. I'm here to help," I whispered.

She played with my hand, holding it close to get a better look at my fingernail, and picked at it gently. Then I scratched her arm. She leaned in. I scratched her shoulder, and she leaned in further. Before long, her eyes were closed, and she had her whole side pressed against the bars of the cage as I busily scratched all her invisible itches. Slowly and carefully, I inserted the needle and injected two ml of antibiotic. Anna pulled back slowly and looked at her shoulder, squinting to search for the invisible flea that dared interrupt her massage. She rubbed the injection site and leaned in again, shifting to let me scratch the bug bite. I rubbed and scratched the coarse fur, slipping the needle into the opposite shoulder and injecting another two ml. Anna looked over, rubbed her arm wonderingly. Then she settled back in, pressing her broad back against the bars. The bug bit her bottom. We repeated this as she continued to present me with itchy parts, periodically looking around for the devious, invisible creepy-crawly, and I continued to inject until she had received her full allotment. Director Li smiled. So did I. Probably the happiest of all was Anna, who, for the next glorious week, received the rest of her antibiotics soothingly paired with a delicious spa massage.

The primate house was not on my regular circuit, but even after she was fully recovered, it was hard to resist dropping by to see my girl. She could pick me out of a crowd in an instant and greeted me with friendly hoots, swinging down to hurry over for a good back scratch.

Michelle was a little surprised when she found out that I was regularly massaging a strong, independent raven-haired beauty with expressive brown eyes, but I assured her she had nothing to fear. My relationship with Anna was strictly platonic—or so I thought.

A few weeks later, Michelle dropped by the zoo.

"You have *got* to meet Anna," I told Michelle excitedly. "She is going to love you."

Chimps develop strong social bonds, and Anna, it turned out, was the jealous type.

"This is my wife," I said to Anna, putting my arm around Michelle and giving her a gentle peck on the cheek as I presented her in front of the cage. Michelle smiled and waved.

"Hello, Anna," she said lovingly. "Paul has told me all about you."

Anna jumped up, screamed, and charged forward, angrily baring her teeth and slapping the ground with all the fire of a jilted lover, piercing Michelle with brown-eyed hatred. Anna was *mad*!

Though she softened somewhat over time, Anna and I never fully recovered from that day. She did not shower me with poop or chocolate milk, but my offers of back-rubs were ignored or met with looks of disdain.

Anna, it turned out, was not a degenerate menace. She was lonely and sad and lashed out at the world in angry frustration. What she needed was love, and to know somebody cared. God offers us both, patiently tolerating our outbursts with heaping doses of grace, patience, and mercy. And it's up to us to pass that on.

Bear with each other and forgive one another if any of you has a grievance against someone. Forgive as the Lord forgave you. Col. 3:13
Then said Jesus, "Father, forgive them; for they know not what they do."
Luke 23:34a

————— ❧ —————

When strangers around us have an inappropriate outburst, we usually react with self-righteous condescension. "That's just rude! There's no need for that kind of behaviour," we say. But when we reach the end of our own rope and lash out angrily at the poor sod who steps on our last un-frayed nerve, we expect patience and understanding. It's a double standard that Jesus addressed in the parable of the unforgiving servant (Matthew 18).

Jesus leads by example, responding to the mocking crowd at the foot of the cross by begging God for mercy for their foolish rebellion. You and I are members of that rebellious crowd as well as recipients of that God-given mercy. Our task is to pass that mercy on, lavishing God's patience and love on those around us, regardless of whether we feel they deserve it. As God's ambassadors, we are to offer love and grace to the world, tangibly demonstrating to others the change that the Holy Spirit has brought about in our own lives—so that they can find him.

————— ❧ —————

Lord Jesus, forgive us for our insolence. For judging others when they fall short of the standard we impose on them, all the while expecting extra doses of grace and understanding when we ourselves fall short. Fill us with your Spirit so that our actions and our reactions reflect your love. Make us trophies of your grace, so that others might see you in us, and be drawn to you. Amen

Thoughts in the Middle of the Night

The bamboo chair creaked beneath me as I lowered myself and tucked the blankets around my snow pants. *Amazing*, I thought, *that I would need snow pants here, in Chengdu.*

It was three a.m., and I was at the zoo. Not for an emergency or because I fell asleep at my desk. I was there for recordkeeping. *Strange time for recordkeeping*, you might think, but there was a reason—an odd one maybe—but a reason none-the-less.

Giraffes give birth standing up, so the babies start life with a six-foot drop. The birth of a big animal, like a giraffe, also involves a *lot* of placental fluid, and, despite my admonition for deep, soft, absorbent straw bedding in the giraffe enclosure, only a sparse sprinkling of stubble covered the concrete to cushion the fall and mop up the fluid. Our little guy had struggled for hours after his free-fall into the world, unable to stand on the slippery concrete floor. We had watched him through the glass, wringing our hands, and willing him to stand. With great effort, he would launch his long neck forward to balance on his chest, struggling and working until he got his spindly back legs adjusted under him. Then, as he paused to catch his breath and prepare for the last big effort, a hind foot would slowly slide sideways and he would crash back down to the ground.

"I can get in there to help him," the giraffe keeper said, tugging on the director's thick down jacket.

Director Li looked at him over her glasses.

"Nope," was all she said—and she was right to say so.

Giraffes have a frighteningly powerful kick, one that can kill a lion—and mothers are famously protective—so for the safety of all involved, she could not allow it.

The little one had struggled for hours before the keeper was able to coax the mother out of the indoor exhibit with fresh greens, allowing others to enter and help the little one up (and add more straw to the enclosure). Reunited, his mother fussed over him, licking with her long blue tongue and nuzzling her little treasure. Then, bending his long neck under her belly, he had tucked in for a hearty, well deserved drink. He had done famously ever since.

That scare, however, started a twenty-four-hour watch during which every minute, literally, of the baby giraffe's day was carefully recorded. This was a good, but exhausting, precautionary measure—at least for that first critical week.

But then someone in authority had decided that these twenty-four-hour watches were so novel, it would be a splendid idea to keep them going for a month. This idea was less well received by the staff, so the vet and keeper departments, which had been pressed into service, took turns relieving the exhausted giraffe keepers during the wee hours of the morning.

And on this cold, dark, damp winter's night, it was my turn. I arrived at work just before three am, driving through the eerily deserted streets of our city. The keeper, sitting on his bamboo chair cocooned in blankets, welcomed me with a bleary-eyed smile and dragged off to bed. The giraffes were inside, with space heaters casting a warm glow at the back of the enclosure. I eased myself into the bamboo chair and started recording.

"Lying down," I noted in the log and looked around.

A minute later, the timer beeped.

"Lying down," I noted again.

Sixty seconds later, "Lying down."

It would be a long night.

At three-thirty, a deep Chinese gong rang from the Buddhist temple next to the zoo. After a period when religion had been banned in China, the temple had been reopened, and monks were being called to prayer in the early morning.

Sitting by a giraffe enclosure in central China, in the dark hours of the morning, wrapped in my many layers of clothing to fight off the damp cold, I reflected on the meaning of life. All over the world, animals (and people) were being born and struggling to live. Wars were being fought, and by graves and in hospitals, loved ones were weeping. In the absence of God, it all seemed so hopeless, so pointless. You are born, you struggle, you die—all is vanity.

However, when you are aware of the loving hand that holds it all together, life is different. Though we may not understand how it all fits together, *he* does. Without God, life is meaningless. But with him, at least the destination, if not the whole path, is clear. Because the destination is God himself.

The little giraffe stood up and wobbled, adorably, toward the fourteen-foot model of splendor and elegant power that was his mother. It was captivating. Tenderness and magnificence all wrapped up in one tableau. The six-foot baby nuzzled his mother, rubbed his face into her long slender neck, and then settled in for a good, long drink. I watched, marveling at the spectacular pair. Surely, we can trust the mind, and the heart, of the God that created such fantastic creatures.

For since the creation of the world God's invisible qualities—his eternal power and divine nature—have been clearly seen, being understood from what has been made, so that people are without excuse"
Romans 1:20

———◦———

Why does a sunset, the Grand Canyon, or a starlit night make us pause, uncontrollably, in silent reverence and awe? Because God, through his creation, is allowing us glimpses of himself, and our recognition of the Creator's fingerprints silence us in wonder. Psychological research has found that awe is a cross-cultural human experience, usually brought on by something in nature, and elicits similar cross-cultural sensations; a diminished sense of self, humility, an expanded sense of time, increased connectedness to others, decreased materialism, a general positive mood and sense of well-being, and a sense of the spiritual.

God has left evidence of himself in nature for all to witness and added specific revelation about himself in Scripture. Nature points to his eternal power and majesty, and Scripture fills us in on the details of his goodness, love, and mercy (among many other things). And all of it leaves us standing, amazed with awe, at the feet of our Creator.

———◦———

Heavenly Father, you who created the vastness of space and the detailed intricacy of our bodies, you know us—and love us anyway. That you know us and care about us as individuals is deeply humbling, Lord. That you, Jesus, would sacrifice yourself on the cross, to restore us rebels to yourself, is absolutely, jaw-droppingly, astonishing. Lord, forgive our pride and inflated sense of self-worth. Lord, restore in us that humble spirit of joy that comes from our relationship with you. In Jesus' name we pray. Amen.

Acknowledgements:

———◉———

I would like to thank my wife Michelle for her love and patience, being married to a man who constantly makes her pause on their walks together in order to inspect a bug, watch a bird, or pet a dog.

I want to thank my kids, Luke, Isaac, Rachel and James for making life a joy and delight. The four of you are God's gift to your mom and I.

Thank you to my incredible editor (you know who you are), for her insightful editing advice and wonderful encouragement, and to John Lewis for his wonderful cover design.

And finally, thank you to God, for the privilege of knowing him, and being loved by him, and being invited to join him in sharing his love with the world.